TRANSFORMING
OUR DAYS

TRANSFORMING OUR DAYS

Spirituality,
Community, and
Liturgy in a
Technological
Culture

RICHARD R. GAILLARDETZ

A Crossroad Book
The Crossroad Publishing Company
New York

The Crossroad Publishing Company
370 Lexington Avenue, New York, NY 10017

Printed in the United States of America

Library of Congress Cataloging-in-Publication Data
Gaillardetz, Richard R., 1958-
    Transforming our days : spirituality, community, and liturgy in a technological culture / by Richard R. Gaillardetz.
      p. cm.
    Contents: The technological shape of daily life – The life of grace – Toward an ecclesial spirituality – Liturgy of the church, liturgy of the world.
    ISBN: 0-8245-1844-6 (alk. paper)
    1. Technology – Religious aspects – Christianity. 2. Christian life. I. Title.
BR115.T42 G35 2000
248.4 – dc21
                                    99-050703

1 2 3 4 5 6 7 8 9 10   06 05 04 03 02 01 00

To Gregory,
who blesses our days!

Contents

Preface

I am not sure when I first began thinking about the relationship between modern technology and the practice of my Christian faith. Most of my work as a professional theologian has focused on the theology of the church, and this book is certainly theological in character. But it was really as a husband and a parent that I came to this topic.

As our family began to grow (my wife, Diana, and I have four young boys) and our lives became more hectic, I gradually sensed a change in the "ecology" of our home. Was it the purchase of a second TV set, a second VCR, the "family" computer, or, first one, then two cell phones? I do remember ruminating about my purchase of a cookbook entitled *Thirty-Minute Meals* and feeling relatively guilty about saying that I baked bread when in fact I was using an automated bread-making machine! All I know is that in spite of the shared commitment of my wife and me to our vocation as parents, something precious in our lives seemed to be seeping out of our family life. Yet even as I knew that this changing ecology was in some way connected to the growing technological "shape" of our lives, a radical repudiation of technology seemed both foolish and futile. No one who has witnessed the demise of polio or tuberculosis, who has traveled to distant locales to explore other cultures, communicated instantaneously with persons across the globe, or researched a project on the Internet can deny the benefits that technology has bequeathed to humanity. An outright dismissal of the benefits of technology made no sense.

Indeed, I am too much a child of technology to ever be able to demonize it. I was raised on Air Force bases and as a youth became infatuated with aerospace technology. Like many a child, I dreamed of becoming a pilot, perhaps even an astronaut. (That was before my eyesight betrayed me and, in some subtle way, redirected me toward the far less exhilarating world of academia.) I worked my way through college as a shift supervisor for a company that built computer semiconductors, and my father and two of my three sisters currently work in the computer industry. Consequently I have lived most of my adult life in a silent and generally unreflective conspiracy with my technological world — willingly enjoying its benefits, but largely ignorant of its dangers.

To some extent I am still engaged in this conspiracy (these words are, after all, being composed on a personal computer). This book is a sustained theological reflection on how technology shapes our lives and how our Christian faith can help us make sense of both the benefits and the risks of living in this technological age. I am not concerned here with the great technological advances that pose obvious ethical dilemmas (for example, nuclear and genetic technologies) but rather with the way technology has not only provided a new template for interpreting our daily lives but has also actually reshaped daily living.

I have been influenced considerably by the work of the social philosopher Albert Borgmann. His analysis of the way in which technology shapes our daily life impresses me as both penetrating and measured. In his three most important books[1] and in numerous articles he has often hinted at the spiritual and theological implications of his analysis. If I make any original contributions in this volume, they lie in trying to bring Borgmann's thought, along with that of several other social commentators, into conversation with a theological reflection on the experience of grace in daily life and the role of the church and its liturgy in opening us up to that transformative experience of grace. For it is my conviction that the challenges that modern technology presents to us are not without their spiritual and theological implications. I hope to demonstrate that modern technology has reshaped our daily existence in ways that can make it difficult to experience the grace of God in our lives.

In chapter 1 I sketch the broad outlines of Borgmann's analysis. By devaluing the more mundane spheres of human life, transforming human goods into mere commodities, relieving us of all "burdens," and assisting us in the mastery of time itself, technology makes it increasingly difficult to be open to the grace and blessings that come to us in our basic human activities.

The technological shape of modern living is often unwittingly sustained by Christian spiritualities that present the experience of God as episodic and occasional. These spiritualities also, at least implicitly, overlook the more mundane human activities as a possible arena for experiencing God's presence. Consequently, in chapter 2 I explore a model of God's interaction with our world, grounded in the doctrine of the Trinity. This model avoids any view of our experience of God as an occasional, episodic, and extrinsic experience — one among many human experiences. Rather, grace is revealed at the heart of human existence, in the ordinary human interactions and worldly engagements that technology too often devalues.

Chapter 3 considers the Christian community as a community of believers that offers in word, action, ritual, and symbol a distinctively Christian account of where and how we might find grace and meaning in our daily lives. In a technological world, membership in a community of believers may be particularly helpful as a means of discerning God's presence in our daily lives.

Finally, chapter 4 presents the Christian liturgy as a privileged activity of the church that helps believers undergo the kind of conversion necessary for discovering God in ordinary human activities and relationships.

This book is far too short to constitute anything like a systematic treatise on the intersection between modern technology and Christian theology and spirituality. What I offer is simply a set of exploratory reflections that might further in some way an important but neglected conversation.[2] Some consider it perfunctory for an author to conclude a preface by acknowledging the debt owed to spouse and family. However, to fail to do so in this instance would constitute not only a breach of etiquette and courtesy but an injustice. For my family has provided the indispensable laboratory for working out all of these reflections. What wisdom may be found herein on the place of technology in our lives emerged out of innumerable family meetings and debates on everything from meal times and menus to appropriate forms of family entertainment. If I have given these insights a certain theoretical veneer, it is my wife, Diana, in particular, who has tempered my excesses and given concrete shape to at least one way of negotiating with our technological world through concrete lifestyle choices. Diana and our four boys, David, Andrew, Brian, and Gregory, have endured more than a few of my diatribes as I worked through my own guilt regarding the gap between the "talk I was talking" (or writing) and the "walk I was walking." It is their firm embrace of the real world that kept me from flying off to utopian extremes.

I would like to thank my colleagues at the University of St. Thomas School of Theology for their companionship and support and Tom Colyandro for the research assistance he offered at the very beginning of this project. I am also grateful for a number of friends and colleagues who graciously read and commented on early versions of this manuscript: Maureen Bacchi, Sandra Derby, Nathan Mitchell, and Jacques

Weber. I owe a distinctive debt of gratitude to Rob Wething, dear friend and kindred spirit, with whom I have shared years of rewarding discussions about both the demands and delights of marriage and family. Finally I should thank Gwendolin Herder and Tom Fenton for their expert editorial assistance in bringing these reflections into publishable form.

Acknowledgments

Permission to quote from the following is gratefully acknowledged:

Albert Borgmann, *Crossing the Postmodern Divide* (Chicago: University of Chicago Press, 1992), with permission of the University of Chicago Press.

Jim Bowman, " 'Missa Latina,' Yes, I Liked It. So Excommunicate Me," *Commonweal* 120 (8 October 1993), with permission of *Commonweal*.

Elizabeth Barrett Browning, "Aurora Leigh," Book VII, with permission of Oxford University Press.

Theodore Jennings, "On Ritual Knowledge," *Journal of Religion* 62 (1982), with permission of the University of Chicago Press.

Norman Maclean, *A River Runs through It* (Chicago: University of Chicago Press, 1976), with permission of the University of Chicago Press.

Karl Rahner, "The Mass and Television," in *The Christian Commitment: Essays in Pastoral Theology* (New York: Sheed & Ward, 1963), with permission of Sheed & Ward, an Apostolate of the Priests of the Sacred Heart, 7373 South Lover's Lane Road, Franklin, WI 53132.

Stephen H. Webb, *The Gifting God: A Trinitarian Ethics of Excess* (New York and Oxford: Oxford University Press, 1996), with permission of Oxford University Press.

Chapter 1

The Technological Shape
of Daily Life

The capture of Theodore Kaczynski, the famed "una-bomber," grasped the imagination of the American public. This fascination is explained in part by the way that his heinous crimes, coupled with the bombings of the World Trade Center in New York, the Murrah Building in Oklahoma City, and at Centennial Park in Atlanta all brought home to the American public the horror of terrorism, which has been a regular feature of life in places like Northern Ireland and the Middle East. However, the terrorist actions of the unabomber are quite distinctive in the tragic paradox they reveal. This zealot, who insisted on the publication of his rambling treatise on the evils of modern technology, could get the attention of the world only by employing that very same technology — constructing letter bombs and publishing his treatise by means of the technological apparatus of the modern media. His condemnation of technology was at the same time a damning act of complicity with modern technology.

The unabomber tragically demonstrates the reasons

why technology can no longer be viewed as a neutral entity that can be used for good or evil. It has entered into the very fabric of our lives. In fact, technology's ability to influence us so profoundly lies in its pervasive "hiddenness"; we are often blind to the subtle ways it shapes our view of, and interaction with, our world.

We look to technology to help alleviate disease, to improve basic human conditions, and, in general, to enhance the quality of our lives. Since the beginning of history, humans have used tools to assist them in providing for their basic human needs. It is tempting to think of the history of technology as the progressive development of ever more complex tools. When we consider the modern computer, for example, does it not appear to us as simply the most sophisticated version of tools for calculation in a history of mechanisms that can be traced back through the slide rule to the abacus? The modern tool may be tremendously more efficient and adaptable than its precursors, but in the end is not modern technology just another instance of humans forging implements to aid the management and improvement of our lives?

One of the foremost contemporary thinkers in the philosophy of technology has made a persuasive case to the contrary. Albert Borgmann contends that technology now operates within a completely different paradigm or framework from that which was typical of the premodern world. This fundamental difference has led to a profound and pervasive reorientation of our lives. The key feature in this shift lies in a distinction Borgmann makes between "focal things" and "devices."

Technological Devices vs. "Focal Things"

Borgmann asks us to consider the role of the fireplace or wood-burning stove in a premodern home. The family frequently gathers around the fireplace as a localized source of heat for important discussion and family entertainment. The fireplace itself must be tended regularly. To do so one must master a set of skills: knowing which kinds of wood burn best and how to properly start and stoke the fire. These skills and practices inevitably bring one into contact with the larger world of nature (retrieving and chopping the wood) and with other persons. They are skills that must be passed on from one person to another. When it is the sole heat source in the home, the fireplace also creates the rhythm for the life of the home. The need for its regular maintenance determines family chores, the timing of meals, the gathering of family and friends.

The fireplace or wood-burning stove is a typical example of what Borgmann calls a "focal thing."[1] Typical "focal things" are inseparable from the particular context in which they are encountered. While they produce a desired good (in this case, heat), they do so only within the context of a complex world of "manifold engagement" — a multitextured, multi-layered web of relationships with the larger world — in which other goods, often overlooked, are also experienced. The wood-burning stove does produce heat, the principal desired good, but it also offers subtler goods derived from the way in which it gathers the household, demands engagement with the larger world, and so forth.

Food is another example. For whether elaborate or simple, the particular context offered in the home preparation of a meal highlights the potentially "focal" character of food. First, in the preparation of a typical meal, one must leave the confines of the home to purchase groceries and produce at the market. To procure fresh produce or meat one must have certain skills. Seasoned cooks know, for example, how to distinguish, by touch and smell, fresh fish from once-frozen or stale fish. They know how to recognize ripe melons. At home a complex orchestration of the various parts of the meal gets underway so that everything is ready at once. The whole family becomes involved — preparing the food, setting the table, serving the food, and cleaning up afterward. Moreover, one of the inevitable by-products of a well-prepared meal is that the considerable time invested in its preparation allows for its leisurely communal enjoyment.[2] Such meals are "focal" because in diverse ways they gather our attention and hold us in patterns of meaningful engagement with others and with the fruit of the earth. The sum is nothing less than a "focal event" and a rich "culture of the table."[3]

A little reflection on these various modes of engagement suggests that the world surrounding the "focal" thing can be seen in ever richer ways. For the skills demanded by the thing (for example, the fireplace, the food to be prepared) provide the opportunity for a certain quality of relationships, as in the tutelary relationship between parent and child. The limits of the thing (for example, fires eventually go out, we run out of food) shape our world; we must leave the home to replenish our supplies. The more we reflect on this manifold engagement the more we can see a vital web of interactions and relationships that constitute one's daily way of life. While focal things are often valued as, or provide, important goods and services, these goods and services are experienced as inseparable from the "world" created by our many engagements with these focal things. This contrasts with the modern technological device.

As an example of a technological device Borgmann proposes the central heating system. It provides the same commodity as the wood-burning stove, namely, heat, but without intruding into our lives or placing demands on our time. Central heating is placed out of sight and runs virtually on its own. We need not understand how it works, it requires no skills (except for the specialists who designed and built it and the technicians who alone can repair it!), it makes no contribution to the rhythms of the day. Indeed, its principal improvement over the fireplace is that it flattens out any rhythm; central heating allows us to stay awake and warm at all hours of the day, unlike a fire that, upon being extinguished, requires family members to seek the warmth of the bed.

In like manner we might consider the way in which the food industry has transformed food from a focal thing into a commodity by means of a myriad of technological devices. This transformation is evident when we attend to the ways in which the modern microwave functions as a device. The use of the microwave oven to prepare a prepackaged microwave dinner requires virtually no engagement with the outer world and no skills, imposes few burdens, requires little time for preparation, and makes no argument for the leisurely consumption of the food.

> Once food has become freely available, it is only consistent that the gathering of the meal is shattered and disintegrates into snacks, TV dinners, bites that are grabbed to be eaten; and eating itself is scattered around television shows, late and early meetings, activities, overtime work and other business. This is, increasingly, the normal condition of technological eating.[4]

Like the focal thing, the modern "device" does offer us vital goods and services, but it does so in a manner that separates the device from the commodity produced. In fact, that device functions best when it goes completely unnoticed, receding into the background. One of the central characteristics of a device is its concealment. It is its concealment that "disburdens" us; the device no longer intrudes on our lives.

A basic thesis of Borgmann's work is that the technological device has become such a pervasive part of our culture that it has now become a "paradigm," that is, it presents a consistent and patterned framework in and through which people encounter their world. As with any overarching model or framework, this paradigm is so pervasive that we are largely blind to the ways in which it influences the way we experience our world. Computers and Internet search engines offer information but without the engagement with the larger world of persons and books demanded by the use of a library or bookstore. The sound entertainment system offers music without musicians and instruments; the exercise treadmill offers us fitness without interaction with the larger world or the cultivation of any discernible set of skills.[5]

What devices rob us of, Borgmann contends, are "focal practices" that are called for by these focal things. These "practices" are often routine ways in which we engage the larger world in our daily lives. They are activities we undertake in order to obtain a desired good, but, and this is crucial, in some sense the goods we desire are internal to the practice — they cannot be separated. These practices, while often pedestrian, generally demand the cultivation of some basic discipline or skill, a certain degree of attentiveness, and they can be judged by some accepted standard of excellence.[6] Provide the good without the practice (for example, food served as a microwave meal rather than prepared "from scratch") and the character of the good itself changes — it becomes a mere commodity. The focal things and events like the fireplace and home-cooked meals require focal practices such as wood-collection, maintenance of the fire, shopping for produce, cutting vegetables, marinating meat, setting the table, and washing dishes after a meal. These focal practices often appear time-consuming and routine. They are predictable and generally devoid of excitement or some distinctive quality that might lead us to privilege them as particularly valued activities. In fact, we often consider such practices mere drudgery. Recall the familiar Mark Twain tale of Tom Sawyer who, when given what he considered the unsavory task of painting a fence on a beautiful Saturday morning, managed to dupe his friends into painting the fence for him by convincing them that whitewashing a fence was indeed a most rare and exciting activity. We catch the humor of the story because we share Tom's conviction that such activities hold no real value. Technology plays on this conviction with the promise that such activities can be efficiently excised from our lives without having to deceive our friends!

The distinctive character of focal practices can be further illuminated when considered under the rubric of "maintenance." Devices discourage maintenance. Many modern devices — the television set, the VCR, the computer — come with warnings not to open the casing. They are not intended to be "maintained" by the consumer. Indeed the high price charged for the professional repair of such devices encourages their replacement rather than their repair! One of the most revered "maintenance" practices in American life has been that of "working on the car." Whole generations of youth were enriched by the tutelary relationship between parent and adolescent established under the hood of a car. Yet the growing role of computerized microprocessors in modern automobile engines and the high-tech diagnostic equipment that their maintenance demands suggests that the days are numbered for fathers and sons "working on a car."

Devices also shape the life of leisure. The preeminent symbol of leisure in a technological society is television. It places no demands, is available all the time, and, with the advent of cable, satellite, and VCR technologies, offers virtually unlimited choice in content. The viewer sits on the couch, selecting at random any of an almost infinite variety of movies, shows, or athletic events, allowing the action on the screen to entertain in a way that encourages the complete passivity of the viewer. Television technology has systematically extracted all forms of human engagement from the entertainment experience. Borgmann insists that the introduction of television into the living rooms of North Americans was not just a case of adding another device or appliance; television has radically reconstituted American life and leisure. Neil Postman makes a similar point when he writes of the "ecological" character of technological change.[7] This is often borne out in the very arrangement of furniture in the modern living room or family room: couches and chairs are often oriented toward the television set rather than being configured in ways more congenial to social interaction.

This analysis suggests the importance of preserving practices of human engagement with one another and with the larger world. When goods are reduced to commodities and procured for enjoyment in ways that do not demand or even allow for real engagement with our world, the paradoxical result is a decreased capacity for enjoyment.[8]

What Borgmann refers to as the "focal" character of things, events, and practices, I will, in the following chapters, consider as a manifestation of "communion." For focal things and practices invite us to abandon a largely instrumental view of our world and its inhabitants in favor of an attitude of "communion" that draws us into attentive, respectful engagement with the larger world. This "communion," I will suggest, finds its ultimate ground in communion with God. However, before developing a theological understanding of the life of communion I would like to explore further the way in which this capacity for authentic celebration, focal living, or "communion," has been threatened by a technological phenomenon that Borgmann calls "hyperreality," a new and seductive way of experiencing reality.

Hyperreality

The term "hyperreality" is borrowed from the Italian philosopher and novelist Umberto Eco.[9] Hyperreality, in effect a synonym for what is more commonly called "virtual reality," is a kind of artificial reality, but an artificial reality that to all appearances is not an impoverishment of reality, some poor facsimile, but an enhancement of reality. Hyperreality has three defining characteristics: it is *brilliant*, that is, it highlights the desirable elements of a given experience while excluding all unwanted aspects; it is *rich* insofar as it is experienced as better than the "real," possessing more than what might "really" be expected from an experience; it is *pliable*, subject to our manipulation and control.[10]

Borgmann gives the example of the contemporary flight simulator used to train military and airline pilots.[11] Not only are contemporary, computerized flight simulators able to duplicate the actual flying experience in remarkable detail, they offer the advantage of "pliability." Twenty years ago airline pilot training would have included numerous training rides in which the pilot, accompanied by a trainer, would have taken a stripped-down airliner to a small nearby airport and there practiced instrument approaches. In a two-hour training flight the pilot might have been able to make five or six extended instrument approaches. These approaches would have been to the same airport however, with minimal opportunity to train under adverse conditions such as poor weather or equipment malfunctions. In that same two-hour period, with a flight simulator, a pilot today can make twice as many approaches. Moreover, in one session he or she can practice approaches at O'Hare, LaGuardia, National, and Dallas–Fort Worth airports. These approaches can be conducted according to any of a number of scenarios in which dangerous malfunctions and hazardous weather conditions can be created to prepare the pilot for the unexpected.

The contrast between the world of the flight simulator and the ordinary training flight illuminates the characteristic features of hyperreality in general. While in "real time" flight training one must learn to submit to the limits of time, "wasting" thirty minutes in travel to and from the local airport, in the "hyperreal time" of the flight simulator time itself becomes subject to control and "wasted" travel time is eliminated. What "real time" offers in a set span of time will always be limited. In "hyperreal time" however, that which is "uneventful," "boring," or "unproductive" can be extracted and replaced with more productive planned experiences. While "real time" blends in subtle and often ambiguous ways the significant and the insignificant, in "hyperreal time" that which is valued as significant is displayed in full brilliance.[12] Hyperreality sharpens the contrast between time in which "things are happening" and dead time in which "nothing is happening." Indeed hyperreality constitutes the technological mastery of time itself.

The Mastery of Time

Hans Bernard Meyer claims that the clock may be the most important machine of modern technology.[13] The influence of the clock in Western civilization is, ironically, closely tied to the monastery and the calling of monks to work and prayer.[14] Until the late thirteenth century, the principal clocks in the monastery were either sundials or water clocks, both of which kept time by careful alignment with the rhythms of the natural order. With the advent of the mechanical clock in the fourteenth century (it was not mass produced, however, until the nineteenth century) time became separated from both the internal (for example, heartbeat, breathing, hunger patterns) and external (for example, the cycle of day and night, the annual seasons) rhythms to which those in premodern times had to align themselves.[15]

Add to the mechanical clock the advent of satellites, the telephone, and supersonic travel and we can see how dramatically modern technology has transformed our experience of time.[16] Once time can be measured in independent units apart from the consideration of internal or external rhythms, it appears to be "under our control." We are encouraged to "make the most of our time," or to "use our time wisely" as if it were one more commodity. As a commodity, time becomes something that must be managed and not wasted. Activities are measured by their time-efficiency. This is the paradox of the hyperreal age perpetuated by the technological device: we are so trapped in an endless spiral to purchase more devices, lured by the promise that they will save us time, that we have lost the ability to "spend" time. We no longer know how to luxuriate in the present because we are obsessed with technologically "banking" our time for some never quite realized future "time of enjoyment."

The modern mastery of time might be considered

from another perspective. Computer technology has given us the notion of "multitasking," the ability to juggle numerous tasks simultaneously. Multitasking allows us to effectively "toggle" back and forth between tasks while the computer keeps the task not being attended to in continuous operation. What it does not do is force us to consider the real relationships that obtain among the various tasks being undertaken. In multitasking we become better "jugglers," but we do not thereby achieve the wisdom that comes from a grasp of the whole. It is no coincidence that "juggling" has become a popular metaphor in our culture for describing our frenetic attempt to maintain control of our lives in the face of increasing fragmentation. To the extent that our technological world encourages multitasking or "juggling," the cramming of greater productivity into discrete units of time, it blinds us to the possibility of multidimensionality, the capacity to experience the flow of time as yielding some only gradually emerging, cumulative insight into the nature of our world.[17]

"A Culture of Simulation"

Already we can recognize other aspects of daily life in which the hyperreal has become so taken for granted that the distinction between the real and the hyperreal is blurred or erased altogether. Music offers a good example. We are now so accustomed to the unique musical perfections provided for us by digitally prerecorded music that it ceases to even occur to many of us that real music might be a matter of "living persons gathering here and now with their tangible instruments, playing together as well as the grace of the hour has it."[18]

One of the most provocative and compelling demonstrations of the phenomenon of hyperreality is offered to us by a corporation that has itself become a kind of American cultural icon, Disney. As anyone who has ever visited either Disneyland or Disneyworld knows, Disney is the unparalleled master in the innovative employment of technology for the construction of authentic, "themed" resorts. Disney's latest creation, the Wilderness Lodge, offers a wonderful example of the pervasiveness and allure of hyperreality in our culture.[19] The Wilderness Lodge, one of several Disney resorts in Orlando, Florida, was created to resemble the turn-of-the-century encounter with the wilderness of the Pacific Northwest. The goal is to immerse the tourist in an experience of the frontier spirit, the beauty and majesty of the wilderness, without the inconveniences that such a "real" encounter would entail: no wilderness skills are required, no hardships endured, no physical vulnerabilities risked. Excluded from the lodge are "unpredictable wild animals" and unplowed, unpaved roads that might break the axle of a vehicle. Geysers go off on predetermined schedules and "guests can peruse native art without having to deal with native people."[20]

I acknowledge the ingenuity and entertainment value of such planned "experiences" (indeed, my own family recently made the American pilgrimage to Orlando!), but we must recognize the way in which these Disney projects technologically blur what counts as "the natural." Is something vital to our experience of the natural order being lost when an experience of "nature" can be sanitized — purged of all inconvenient elements?

Sherry Turkle's masterful study of the psychological and sociological impact of Internet technologies further illuminates aspects of hyperreality. For example, she has observed in the history of computer technology a shift from "a culture of calculation toward a culture of simulation."[21] Whereas in the early years of computer technology we saw the computer as simply an immensely powerful calculator, the most interesting uses for computers today are not those requiring calculation but those that enable an increasingly elaborate simulation of what we hitherto counted as "real."

This culture of simulation is evident in the burgeoning popularity of interactive video and computer games that has grown out of the television culture. The interactivity of these games is often presented as an advance over the passivity of television watching. To be sure, this interactivity can easily be mistaken for authentic human engagement. The most advanced interactive computer games, such as Myst, its successor Riven, or any in the Sim series (for example, Simcity, Simlife), allow players to explore and/or create their own "worlds." They make choices that redefine the contours of the game itself.[22] In a sense, every game is completely different. One gets the impression of being an actor, a participant in the particular game as it is programmed to react to and accommodate the player's choices. But this interaction is deceptive, for whatever can be said for the quality of "interaction" offered by such games, it is not an encounter with another "self," another person possessing mysterious depths. "Interaction" is no replacement for interpersonal, human engagement.[23]

There can be no doubt of the remarkable gains that Internet technologies have made in the acquisition, management, and exchange of information. The world of academic scholarship is being transformed, with new tools for research being developed. Significant business can now be transacted without partners actually having to meet with one another, saving valuable time. Shopping, once itself a common social activity, can now be done more effectively on the Internet, taking advantage of huge inventories impossible to maintain in conventional stores. Yet while the advances in Internet technologies have offered us incredible convenience and the greatly expanded accessibility of the goods we desire, they have also robbed us of some of the most basic contexts for daily human engagement: for example, browsing with a friend in stores or discussing a research project with a librarian.

A significant social consequence of this new reality is the phenomenon often referred to as "cocooning" as Americans find less and less reason to leave their home and interact with any but a small circle of family, friends, and associates. Certainly, the blame for cocooning cannot be placed at the feet of Internet technologies alone. As the advocates of New Urbanism have long pointed out, much of the blame lies with poor urban planning, the banal sprawl of suburban life, and the emergence of the shopping mall. Cumulatively, these factors have deprived us of those vital places for human gathering (for example, taverns, city parks, cafes, or general stores) romantically evoked in the televisions series *Cheers*, "where everybody knows your name." Ray Oldenburg laments the passing of these traditional places for human interaction, what he refers to collectively as the "third place" for forming human community (the first two being work and home).[24]

Howard Rheingold, however, has boldly proposed that "virtual communities" formed on the Internet may be a new kind of "third place."[25] While the opportunities for and interest in face-to-face human interaction are contracting, the possibilities for global communication via the Internet are expanding exponentially. The Internet allows us to engage conversation partners around the globe about matters of common interest. The flourishing of newsgroups, chatrooms, and computer conferencing offers examples of the Internet's potential for creating new forms of virtual community. Rheingold contends that these new forms of community are a liberation of sorts for those who consider themselves shy and who suffer in social situations. These individuals flourish in virtual communities in which their computer screen provides a buffer, allowing them to think through what they wish to communicate.

For them the seemingly artificial mode of communication mediated by the Internet is in fact more authentic than the awkward and forced exchanges at more conventional social engagements. Moreover, for those who live in remote locations or who are physically disabled, virtual communities offer a vital social lifeline.

One of the unique features of this new form of "virtual community" derives from the peculiarly disembodied character of the virtual interaction. Howard Rheingold's description of such "virtual communities" admits this:

> People in virtual communities use words on screens to exchange pleasantries and argue, engage in intellectual discourse, conduct commerce, exchange knowledge, share emotional support, make plans, brainstorm, gossip, feud, fall in love, find friends and lose them, play games, flirt, create a little high art and a lot of idle talk. People in virtual communities do just about everything people do in real life, *but we leave our bodies behind.*[26]

Nothing better illustrates both the seductiveness and the danger of such disembodied interaction than the newest entry among the various manifestations of "virtual community," the MUD, or Multi-User Domain.[27] The inspiration for MUDs seems to have come from the fantasy game "Dungeons and Dragons" and its many variants. MUDs represent a "virtual parlor game" in which participants become characters of their own making, interacting in a given setting with other players or "bots" (artificial intelligence programs that function as a player's alter ego, continuing limited interaction with other characters while the player is otherwise engaged, or serving as a permanent complement to the "real" players). Many participants will maintain multiple identities in different MUDs. Here participants find an exhilarating opportunity to explore new identities, often assuming attitudes and patterns of behavior seldom displayed in their "real lives." Participants will frequently construct assumed identities of a different gender.

Of course, this process of disembodiment is not altogether new. In the past, relationships conducted through written correspondence or telephone conversation also had a somewhat disembodied character. But then relatively few of those relationships were sustained *entirely* by written or telephone communication, and, in the latter case, one had at least the sound of a human voice as a vestige of some embodied presence. Moreover, while it was possible to deceive a pen pal with fictitious information about one's self, this was seldom *presumed* as it is with MUDs. MUDs and chatrooms allow people to offer "stylized versions of themselves for amorous or convivial entertainment."[28] One can only wonder whether, over time, these fictitious identities will bleed into other related forms of Internet communication such as e-mail, further blurring the boundaries between what is "real" and what is "virtual." This blurring is due in no small part to the diminished need for embodied presence.

Yet embodied presence is vital to authentic interpersonal engagement because it is our embodiment
that creates the conditions for both separateness from
another and presence to another. When I am bodily
present to another there is an intrinsic vulnerability.
Whether I am aware of it or not, I am always com-
municating through innumerable verbal and nonverbal
cues either more or less than I intend. But this embodiment is simply "bracketed out" in "chatroom" or
MUD participation. As Michael Heim puts it, the electronic medium allows us to "reveal only as much of
ourselves as we mentally wish to reveal."[29] This lack
of embodiment is less apparent in the more advanced
virtual reality technologies that employ digitized, electronic representations of the embodied self (the current
state of such technologies was displayed to the aver-
age layperson in the Michael Crichton novel and film
Disclosure). However, even this electronic, corporeal
surrogate is incapable of mediating anything of "the
vulnerability and fragility of our primary identity."[30]
Such technologies offer the participant a voyeuristic
semblance of intimacy without the vulnerability. It is
easy to understand how Heim can write of the "erotic
ontology of cyberspace."[31]

Finally, we might note the role of the modern media
in the construction of hyperreality. Largely because of
the shift from the printed medium to the visual medium
of television, the line between "reporting" the news
and "manufacturing" it has become blurred, if it has
not disappeared altogether. It is precisely the "rich-

ness," the "brilliance," and the "pliability" of modern television that allows the TV journalist to rely on the overwhelming cacophony of visual images to tell a compelling story. What "really" happened has become almost irrelevant. This was clearly the point of the film *Mad City*, in which a TV journalist cynically manipulates a disgruntled former museum employee who had taken hostages in the museum to protest his firing. By befriending the former employee and becoming the "arbitrator" between him and the authorities, the journalist created a media "event."

Michael Crichton makes a similar point in his novel *Airframe*, describing the media's resistance to reporting the truth about a commercial airline "incident" in favor of using sensational video footage of passengers being mangled and killed during the in-flight "incident." Near the end of the novel, one of the characters, having witnessed the way the media has come to deal with airline accidents and their investigations, makes the following observation:

> "Fact is," Amos said, "everything's changing. Used to be — in the old days — the media image roughly corresponded to reality. But now it's all reversed. The media image is the reality, and by comparison day-to-day life seems to lack excitement. So now day-to-day life is false and the media image is true. Sometimes I look around my living room, and the most real thing in the room is the television. It's bright and vivid, and the rest of my

life looks drab. So I turn the damn thing off. That
does it very time. Get my life back."[32]

This description of day-to-day life as "lacking excitement" sums up well the effect of hyperreality on
modern existence.

The Indispensable Role of "Friction" in Our Lives

One might ask whether this extended jeremiad against
hyperreality is not in the end little more than a kind of
nostalgia for what is ultimately a less satisfying body
of human goods? Why insist on the significance of this
distinction between the real and the hyperreal when
the sensory input of the real can be perfectly emu-
lated and even enhanced by hyperreality (as is the case
with recorded music)? Why not simply take advantage
of hyperreality's promise to provide more accessible
and convenient enjoyment of those things which we
most value?

By way of an answer, I would like to consider a
thought experiment proposed by Borgmann. Imagine
a professional living in western Montana who loves
the outdoors and has a set of treasured trails that she
regularly runs. She is offered a lucrative position in
the Midwest. Knowing that she loves to run outdoors,
her prospective employers sweeten the deal by offering
her a membership in a special health club that features
treadmills with videotapes for runners to watch while
jogging. Now admittedly this artificial environment
would be a poor facsimile of the real thing. A glance

in either direction would reveal other health club members, not wilderness, and the smells and sounds would be those of the gym, not of nature. But what if modern technology allowed us to greatly improve the facsimile? What if we could use a state of the art projection screen, add temperature-controlled blowers and the appropriate sounds and scents? Now the professional might find this enhanced hyperreal encounter truly captivating, a novelty to share with friends. Borgmann writes:

> Consider once more the case with which we began. The professional woman, after a most stressful morning, is running in her favorite winter landscape. New snow is sparkling in the sun, yet the footing is perfect. Snow geese are vigorously rising from the river. Then it is quiet but for the scolding of the Steller's jays. A snowshoe hare up ahead is hopping along the trail. There, suddenly, is a crashing in the brush, a gigantic leaping and pouncing; a mountain lion has taken the hare and is loping back up the slope. Quiet once more settles on the valley. A herd of elk is browsing in the distance. The trail is rising. The runner is extending herself; she reaches the crest of the incline; another quarter mile and the trailhead comes into view.[33]

Borgmann asks if it really matters whether this run took place in the real setting or in a hyperreal facsimile. We might be tempted to dismiss the difference as long as the sensory experience was exactly reproduced. But this would be a mistake.

Assume the woman is coming to the end of her run. She walks past the trailhead to the parking lot, gets in her car and drives down the snowy valley to her office. She is elated. People spend years in the mountains without ever seeing a lion. To see one at the height of a hunt is a rare blessing. And she feels blessed also to live in a region wide and wild enough to support mountain lions, and on a continent hospitable enough for geese to nest in the North and winter in the South. She revels in the severity of the early winter that has driven the snow geese south from Canada and the elk down from the high country. The snow must already be ten feet deep on the peaks and ridges. There will likely be a heavy runoff in the spring and strong river flows throughout the summer. This is where she wants to be.

Assume once more the woman is coming to the end of her run. The vista is dimming, the running surface is slowing down, the ceiling lights are coming on. She goes to the locker room, showers, changes, and steps into a muggy, hazy afternoon in the high-rise canyon of a big city. All that was true of the real run would now be false. The hyperreal run would have revealed nothing about her surroundings, would have bestowed no blessings on

her, and would not have been an occasion for her
to affirm her world.[34]

This provocative thought experiment brings into
sharp relief the full moral force of Borgmann's analysis of technology and the hyperreality that it generates.
Sensory input may be perfectly re-created, but lost in
that "perfect" re-creation is the mysterious lure of the
unknown and the unpredictable. These appear only
when we abandon attempts to master time and instead wade into the flow of time and submit to its
current. The very brilliance and complete accessibility
of modern technology actually undermine our experience of the ordinary world. For a discovery of the
ordinary world includes not only epiphanies and reve-
lations but the apprehension of ambiguities, distances,
and hidden horizons which can never be immediately
accessible to us.

Dangerously, many technological advances rob human existence of "friction." Yet the experience of
friction is one of the essential qualities that gives ordinary human existence texture — it is what makes
our existence "real."[35] It is precisely the "rough fit,"
the "mixed bag" of so many human interactions that
brings freshness and vitality to our lives. I mean no dis-
respect to my wife when I say that it is the friction in our
relationship, the ambiguous messages, the gentle jibes,
the fights and reconciliations, the resentments over
what is withheld and the gratitude for what is given —
all of it — which constitutes the substance of what is

lively and life-giving in our marriage. Within a total-
ized technological perspective human experience itself
becomes truncated. The demand for imaginative engagement and a stance of receptivity, attentiveness, and
openness to the world as it alternatively displays and
veils itself is superseded by the imaginatively brilliant
construct of the software designer. In such a technological, hyperreal world, I can no longer be "surprised
by joy." Max Frisch can be excused for a bit of hyper-
bole when he remarked, "technology is the knack of so
arranging the world that we do not experience it."[36]

The reader may be tempted to ask, at this point,
whether technological devices and experiences of
hyperreality must always be bad. Indeed, the problem
could be posed something like this: Even if I recognize
the deleterious impact of technology on my daily life,
I must also acknowledge the many benefits it brings.
These are advances that, quite frankly, I am not sure I
wish to surrender. It is quite romantic to evoke images
of home-cooked meals, families gathered around the
hearth listening to the storytelling of the elders, and
long, leisurely runs in picturesque canyons. Yet for
many modern families, particularly single-parent or
two-income families struggling to keep the family ship
afloat, the desire for the recovery of focal things and
practices in service of a focal or "eloquent reality"
(Borgmann's term) may seem an unaffordable luxury.
Many families are so overwhelmed by the daunting
task of getting everyone fed, clothed, and off to school
on time that they have little opportunity to schedule

in a weekly trip with the kids to the farmers' market to hand pick organically grown produce! Moreover, few people old enough to recall the harsh realities of knuckles rubbed raw washing clothes on a washboard would be willing to dispense with the modern washing machine. In short, how does all of this help me navigate in a technological world I cannot ever really escape? Is there an alternative to the tendency to demonize technology so evident in many approaches to the subject?

Here again, I have found Borgmann's own approach instructive. He admits that it is futile to try and completely dismantle the technological paradigm. Rather, what we must seek is a realistic and measured reform of the paradigm. What is required is conscious reflection on one's life with a view toward identifying and cultivating vital focal practices. The conscious identification and preservation of focal practices will help restrain the device paradigm, keeping the employment of devices within their proper sphere, namely, the service of the focal practices that bring meaning and grace to our lives.[37] After all, our principal difficulty is not technology itself but our inability to differentiate between the central life practices that we wish to preserve because they bring meaning and grace and those spheres of life for which efficiency and cost-benefit analysis properly ought to reign.

But such reform cannot be easy. Because we are not just making choices about particular technologies but rather about the overall shape of our lives, the kind of discernment called for here is particularly demanding. In a recent essay Borgmann warned that a "culture informed by the device paradigm is deeply inhospitable to grace and sacrament."[38] For that very reason, I believe that the Catholic Christian tradition's sacramental view of the world and, in particular, the conviction that ordinary human activities and relationships are a privileged place for the encounter with God, can help us cultivate the skills of discernment necessary to negotiate successfully the demands that this technological age places on us. The rest of this volume will address the ways in which the distinctive wisdom of the Christian tradition, its stories, rituals, and actions, can help effect this reform and bring about the recovery of a richer, more vital, and graceful way of living.

Chapter 2

The Life of Grace

The last chapter drew on the work of Albert Borgmann as part of an extended reflection on the characteristic shape of modern living in a technological world. But is Borgmann simply calling us to a more meaningful or "eloquent" human existence? Or can his plea be further illuminated by reference to the Christian life of grace and discipleship? In this chapter I will suggest that there are Christian resources within our tradition that support the call to preserve vital focal things and practices in our daily life. Principal among these theological resources are Christian understandings of the doctrine of the Trinity and a theology of grace.

Reflections on Trinitarian Faith

The Christian tradition considers the doctrine of the Trinity one of its central teachings. One might assume, therefore, that any spirituality that goes by the name Christian would be grounded in the doctrine of the Trinity. I am inclined to believe, however, that much the opposite is the case. In fact, much popular Christian spirituality is more "unitarian" in character. That is,

Christians tend to imagine a relatively undifferentiated God whom they simply name variously, Father, Son, or Spirit. As we will see, imagining God in this way actually encourages a view of our relationship with God as a set of distinct experiences of God's presence set alongside the many more profane or "godless" experiences of our daily life. By neatly dividing our life into religious moments and secular or profane moments, this view, I contend, actually reinforces that technological view of daily life discussed in the last chapter that dismisses much of daily living as boring, insignificant, and burdensome.

Let us consider two alternative spiritual frameworks and the understandings of God that they presuppose.[1] These two frameworks or models might be called, first, unitarian or solitary theism and, second, trinitarian or relational theism.

Unitarian or "Solitary" Theism

The unitarian or solitary theist view of God tends to emphasize the distinction and distance between God and the world. God is conceived as an individual being who is bigger, better, and more powerful than ourselves, but an individual being nonetheless. The alternative, which actually differs little, is that God is viewed as a community of *three* individual beings, one of whom we will tend to address in prayer. In either case, God will always be another individual being "out there somewhere" (see figure 1 on the following page).

I believe this to be the common view of God even

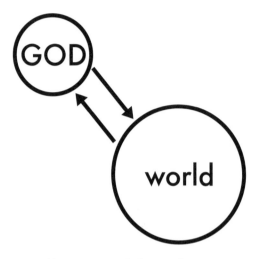

Unitarian or Solitary Theism

for the majority of Christians who profess orthodox trinitarian doctrine. It is quite possible to have our language say one thing while we continue to act out of an alternative imaginative framework.

This unitarian framework, I believe, actually dominates the religious imagination of most Christians today.[2] It has been reinforced by a philosophical approach to God that emerged gradually several centuries ago. With the rise of modern science people no longer needed to appeal to God to explain natural events like the movement of the planets or weather patterns. Modern science seemed to make God irrelevant for understanding our world. What was left was an image of God as the divine "clockmaker." God first creates that great clock, which is our universe, and then stands back to allow the clock to mark time on its own, intervening only occasionally to make the necessary adjustment of the hands.

Two practical consequences follow from this unitarian theism. First, if God is an individual being among other individual beings, another individual in the "larger household of all reality," as the Catholic theologian Karl Rahner put it,[3] then God will inevitably have to compete for my love and attention. My whole life will be an endless tug-of-war between the matters that demand my attention in the daily course of human affairs — preparing classes, buying groceries, playing with my children, talking with my wife — and my religious obligations to God. Regrettably, in Catholic thought theologies of committed celibacy still assume this perspective and consequently suggest that the committed celibate, free from the "distractions" of marriage and family, is better able to love God.

Second, because in this view God is an individual outside my ordinary world, my encounter with God will depend on some kind of episodic intervention. I encounter God only in response to prayer or through the reception of the sacraments or some such thing. My life is construed as essentially profane and godless, punctuated by brief encounters with the sacred. In consequence, the spiritual life will be a mad attempt to insert as many "sacred" moments as possible into the profane structure of daily life hoping thereby to sanctify that life. This "episodic" spirituality in turn leads to the "thingification" of grace, that is, the tendency to imagine divine grace as a kind of spiritual fuel, and the church and its ministers as sacramental grace dispensers.

At this point, it is worth noting the congeniality of this unitarian view of God and the spirituality it engenders to the account of technology's impact on how we experience daily life, as we discussed in chapter 1. Consider again the peculiar logic of technological devices. One way to describe how they shape our lives is to speak of the "commodification of goods." By this I mean the extraction of a particular good from the context in which it is produced, such that this good can now be quantified and measured, making it subject to economic exchange, manipulation, and control. When goods become commodities, the good is stripped of its particularity, the way in which its "goodness" is derived, in part, from the particular context out of which it emerges.

Let me offer an example from my childhood. One of the prized pastimes of my youth involved collecting baseball cards. My father was a Red Sox fan and so I grew up a Sox fan as well. Thus, I always sought to collect cards of my Red Sox heroes both from the past (for example, Ted Williams) and the present (for example, Carl Yastrzemski). These cards were symbols of my undying allegiance to the Red Sox, tangible connections to hours spent watching baseball games with my father. Baseball cards are still quite popular. Indeed, an industry has grown around them. At huge baseball memorabilia expos you can ascertain the worth of your cards and engage in exchange. We exchanged baseball cards when I was a child, but there were always some cards that I insisted on keeping. Today, however, children appear to have little personal attachment to the cards. The baseball card has for many become reduced to a commodity, and the value of one's collection is determined by a professional collector and not by the wealth of memories and dreams that perusing the collection evokes. As I am using the term then, a commodity is a good that lacks context, a particular framework that gives it value; it is now packaged, mobile, subject to my manipulation, control, and exchange.

The technological device turns goods into commodities. Returning to Borgmann's example, a home-cooked meal is a good that is rich in context — it cannot be separated from the activities and interactions that transpired from supermarket to kitchen to dinner table, all necessary for the good of this meal to be realized. The microwave meal, on the other hand, is for the most part a good turned into a commodity — it has no particularity, no context. Every package with the same label is essentially the same meal.

I believe that this commodification of goods has been extended to the religious sphere in our age. Episodic spirituality — in which religious experience is simply a subset of human experience, placed alongside other kinds of experiences — says something about the contemporary packaging of grace. In this technological world, the spiritual seeker often turns to "technique" to encounter the transcendent, whether it be some form of meditation or through a particular dietary discipline. In this way, religious experience is assigned its proper "place" together with the other commodified experiences of our world. Religion becomes a commodity that can be prepackaged so as to fit into our busy lives.

Examples of this abound in so-called "New Age" religion, but let me add similar examples from fringe traditionalist groups in the Roman Catholic tradition. In an op-ed piece in *Commonweal* Jim Bowman wrote of his experience at a liturgy of the Society of Saint Pius X (associated with the late schismatic Archbishop Marcel Lefebvre):

> These are traditionalist Catholics who reject Vatican II as the work of freemasons and Protestants and running-dog liberals. For them the Mass says it all. If it isn't Tridentine . . . it's not a Mass. That's not my position, but I like their Mass. It has Latin and Gregorian music and incense and long periods when we pewsitters have nothing to do but let the music and smell of incense and overall ambiance of set-piece reverence wash over us. At the kiss of peace, we do not turn to shake hands with our neighbors — the virtual highlight of the Masses I usually attend. Instead we concentrate on God above. . . . I count myself a modern churchgoer, but my baptism did not entirely take as a member of the new church, it seems. For one thing, I relish the passivity of this worship experience. No song leader is up there waving and weaving in

order to help me to be a good Catholic by singing up a storm. No celebrant looking me in the eye, sometimes like a veritable talk-show host, eliciting (extorting?) my response to his "The Lord be (or is) with you." No neighbor in the pew is looking for my hand at the Lord's Prayer. None turns to me at the handshake of peace. I'm alone with God and I love it.[4]

Here we have a description of religious experience that is radically divorced from all human, communal contexts. God has been injected into this man's world by way of incense and bells.

Yet at its heart, is not the doctrine of the incarnation the fundamental subversion of this radical separation of the sacred and the profane? Did not Jesus Christ come, not just to save individual souls, but to redeem the world? As I hope to demonstrate, the retrieval of an authentic trinitarian spirituality challenges this separation of the sacred and the profane, along with the commodification of grace. We need a new understanding of the life of grace that resists both the technological tendency to turn all human goods into commodities and the allure of hyperreality that might encourage us to excise the "down time" in our lives when nothing seems to be "happening."

Trinitarian or "Relational" Theism

Though one can certainly find instances of unitarian spirituality within the mainstream Christian tradition,

I believe that there is an alternative model of God's relations with humanity. This model imagines God not as another individual being competing for our attention but as the loving and creative ground of our existence, the very atmosphere in whom we "live and move and have our being" (Acts 17:28). It is a model rooted in an appreciation of the basic insights of trinitarian doctrine. The doctrine of the Trinity has been for so long neglected in Christian life because in popular thought it has been viewed as an insoluble arithmetic problem — how can 3 equal 1? This view misses the insight of trinitarian doctrine completely.

We need a more dynamic perspective that imagines God neither as an individual nor as three individuals bound together in some way, but rather as a pulsing, divine movement toward us in love. Long before trinitarian doctrine became formalized in the definitions of the early ecumenical councils, the church possessed a lived trinitarian faith in which God was encountered precisely as a dynamic movement toward humanity in the life of love. The formal doctrine of the Trinity simply gave formal expression to the way in which Christians experienced this God in history and preeminently in Jesus of Nazareth. Conceiving the triune life of God as a dynamism of divine love reflects the essential insight of trinitarian doctrine, namely, that God's very being, what it is for God *to be,* is loving, life-giving relationality. God does not just *have* a love relationship with us, God *is* loving relationality. There is no self-contained, divine individual residing in heaven far

Trinitarian or Relational Theism

away from us; there is simply a dynamic movement of divine love, which *is* God. Greek Orthodox bishop and theologian John Zizioulas describes this trinitarian vision of God as Being-as-Communion.[5] This model suggests an alternative way of conceiving the life of grace, a vision of God's way of being present with us that is revealed in the fundamental doctrine of the Christian faith, the Trinity (see figure 2).

Our understanding of the doctrine of the Trinity, however, does not end with God, for the doctrine of the Trinity also implies something important about ourselves as well. We have been created in the image and likeness of God. This means that something is written within our very being that binds us to God. This is, I believe, our own limited but real capacity for human relationship, for communion. Just as in God's very essence God is loving relationality, Being-as-Communion, so too we are invited to discover ourselves in the life of communion. Just as God is no self-contained individual being, so too, each of us, as persons created in the image and likeness of God, is not a self-contained individual. We discover our true identity as persons only when we abandon the secure cocoon of a privatized existence and reach out to attend to the world around us. When we stand in awe of the wonders of God's creation, when we find ourselves grasped by a piece of music or a beautiful painting, we experience a kind of self-forgetfulness that draws us beyond ourselves into communion with our larger world. In this movement we become, however imperfectly, personal beings-in-communion — we are living the life of communion.

In a particularly profound way we realize the life of communion when we attend to other persons as creatures possessing an infinite worth and dignity. It may be something dramatic and monumentally difficult, as in forgiving our enemies, or it may be something as simple as making sustained eye-contact with a convenience store clerk. These are all acts of communion.[6]

This life of communion finds a wonderful exploration, albeit in different terminology, in the thought of Hasidic philosopher and theologian Martin Buber.[7] According to Buber, there is no autonomous "I" or self, but rather only persons in relation. Furthermore, as persons in relation, only two basic kinds of rela-

tion are possible: I-It, and I-Thou. The I-It relation is
that quality of relation in which we objectify the world
around us, placing everything into distinct categories —
in short, in the I-It relation, we impose order on our
world. Now the I-It relation is not a bad thing. In fact it
is absolutely necessary if we are going to function in this
world. As a teacher, on the first day of school, I walk
into the classroom and immediately categorize those
seated in the room as "students." It is this kind of basic
categorization that allows us to function in our world
and it certainly has its place. However, Buber contends
that we humans have a unique capacity to transcend
the I-It relation and enter into another kind of relation,
what he calls the I-Thou relation. In the I-Thou relation I no longer seek to objectify the world, making
it accessible for manipulation and control by putting
people and things into their respective categories, but
rather I forget myself in moving out to the world in a
stance of attentiveness. Here I simply become present to
the world around me; I become vulnerable, receptive,
to what the world has to offer. The I-Thou relation
is possible in my engagement with creation itself, but
it is manifested in a particularly dramatic way in an
encounter with another human person. In the interpersonal I-Thou encounter the other person becomes
a subject possessing mysterious depths, a person to be
encountered, not controlled.

Let us consider a rather common event from daily
life. Let us imagine that I am visiting a local Mc-
Donald's. As I walk into the store, either relation is

possible. If I do what I normally do, I will walk into the door and as I approach the counter my eyes are already fixed on the menu overhead. I am greeted by the employee, but my eyes never leave the menu and I begin to rattle off my order. Two minutes later, I have my food and the restaurant has my money. This is a classic I-It encounter. My encounter with the employee on the other side of the counter was no more than a functional transaction not much different than if I were using a vending machine. But let us say that instead, as I walk into the store and am greeted by the employee, I stop, look her in the eye, and offer a greeting in return. In that momentary exchange I note that she is likely a new employee. She seems nervous. As she takes my order I see her struggling to enter the proper code into the electronic register as an impatient supervisor hovers near by. Moreover, I note her overall haggard demeanor; she is middle-aged and unlikely to have the energy of her school-age co-workers. I wonder if she is a single mother, if this is her second job. Do I detect a fleeting glimpse of despair in her eyes? She hands me my food and I her money and as we wish each other a good day, I allow my eye contact to linger a fraction longer than I normally would and hope, perhaps in vain but perhaps not, that in it she sees understanding and compassion. This is a moment in the life of communion.

This life of communion is more than just an imitation of Christ. When we engage in the life of communion, when we move beyond ourselves to attend to the world around us in an event of communion, when we orient ourselves to the needs and concerns of others, we are being drawn by the Holy Spirit into the divine life of God. This is one of the most radical convictions of authentic trinitarian faith. Recall that within the functional unitarian perspective God as individual competes with the other concerns in our lives for attention and love. In an authentic trinitarian faith, however, God does not compete with my love for my wife and children. God is not an alternative to my attending to the McDonald's employee. In my entrance into communion with others and the world around me I am simultaneously drawn into communion with God who makes all love, all authentic relationship possible. This lies at the heart of Jesus' message regarding the unity of the first two commandments, love of God and love of neighbor, and it is developed in the mystical love tradition of the Johannine epistles:

> No one has ever seen God. Yet, if we love one another, God remains in us, and his love is brought to perfection in us. This is how we know that we remain in him and he in us, that he has given us of his Spirit. . . . God is love, and whoever remains in love remains in God and God in him. (1 John 4:12, 13, 16b)

Note that it is the Holy Spirit dwelling within us who is the source of all love. In the practice of trinitarian spirituality it is not necessary to inject God into our everyday lives because in every event of loving communion the Spirit of God is already present, rising up within us as both the source and the goal of all love and the interior principle and agent of all authentic communion.

When we imagine God as a solitary individual, grace often becomes a kind of supernatural "stuff" and the life of grace becomes a matter of petitioning God as frequently as possible to bring this "spiritual fuel" into our lives. Churches, and even the sacraments and the liturgy, as we will see in chapter 4, can become technological devices that give us this spiritual fuel on demand. However, a whole new way of conceiving of the life of grace follows from this trinitarian perspective. "Communion" is, in this context, another word for grace. In other words, grace is not so much a divine substance as it is a quality of relation in which the presence of God emerges as we attend to the world around us and receive it as gift. Grace manifests itself whenever we give ourselves over to the way of love. If God is love, and grace is the presence of God in our midst, then grace is a word we give to what happens to us whenever we are drawn into communion with God and God's creation. Quite simply, the life of communion *is* the life of grace.

While this notion of "communion" is not identical to the focal practices described by Borgmann, there are significant resonances between the two notions. For the life of communion, like focal practices, demands an attitude of attentiveness and active engagement with the world and its inhabitants. Just as focal practices resist turning goods into commodities, so too the life of communion recognizes that grace cannot be commodified. It can neither be earned through pious works nor received mechanistically through either the ministrations of the church or some kind of spiritual "technique."

The rest of this volume will presume this relational theism as the context for further reflection. I believe it is the only adequate theological framework for confronting the tendency of our technological world to transform basic human goods into commodities and to devalue the many mundane engagements and activities that comprise our daily lives. I am further convinced that Christianity (though not necessarily Christianity alone) possesses the theological resources necessary to challenge these features of our technological world. But marshaling these resources requires the development of both a mystagogy of daily life and a renewed Christian asceticism.

A New "Mystagogy"

Authentic Christian spirituality insists that the encounter with grace does not happen by acquiring the goods we desire in ever more efficient and effortless ways through technological devices and hyperreal existence. Rather it invites us to see that it is the very ordinary activities, practices, and engagements that technology often strives to eliminate as burdensome and unnecessary that can become mediations of grace, occasions of divine blessing. This attentiveness might well begin by plumbing the mystery of creation itself. Annie Dillard, the Pulitzer award-winning naturalist whose writings are remarkable for their shimmering spirituality, observes:

> Our life is a faint tracing on the surface of mystery, like the idle, curved tunnels of leaf miners on the face of a leaf. We must somehow take a wider view, look at the whole landscape, really see it, and describe what's going on here. Then we can at least wail the right question into the swaddling darkness, or, if it comes to that, choir the proper praise.[8]

More often than not it is the poet who presents to us the divine mystery disclosed in creation, whether it be Gerard Manley Hopkins's portrait of a world "charged with the grandeur of God,"[9] or the evocative biblical allusion to Moses and the burning bush in Elizabeth Barrett Browning's narrative poem, *Aurora Leigh:*

> Earth's crammed with heaven,
> And every common bush afire with God;
> But only he who sees, takes off his shoes —
> The rest sit round it and pluck blackberries
> And daub their natural faces unaware
> More and more from the first similitude.
> If a man could feel,
> Not one day, in the artist's ecstasy,
> But everyday, feast, fast, or working-day,

The spiritual significance burn through
The hieroglyphic of material shows,
Henceforward he would paint the globe with
    wings,
And reverence fish and fowl, the bull, the tree,
And even his very body as a man.... [10]

Among theologians, perhaps no one has done more to highlight the graced character of every aspect of human existence than Karl Rahner. Rahner's transcendental analysis of human existence led him to reject any extrinsic theology of grace as a merely episodic intervention of God in a profane world. Rahner affirmed that in the basic dynamisms of the human spirit in questioning, loving, hoping, and acting, God was always already present as Holy Mystery. God is the absolute depth and infinite horizon of any truly human experience.[11] While known for his often dense and even opaque philosophical theology, Rahner could write movingly of God's luminous presence in the human experiences of loneliness, the courageous acceptance of death, the unconditional offer of forgiveness, and the sheer delight of human laughter. Rahner was convinced that the very future of Christianity depended on its ability to bring the ordinary believer to an appreciation of the presence of mystery in daily living:

The Christian of the future will be a mystic or he or she will not exist at all. If by mysticism we mean, not singular para-psychological phenomena, but

a genuine experience of God emerging from the
heart of existence, this statement is very true and
its truth and importance will become still clearer
in the spirituality of the future.[12]

Following the lead of Rahner, I suggest that what we
need today is a new "mystagogy"[13] in which humankind is guided to a more profound recognition of the
presence of God as Holy Mystery emerging from within
the warp and woof of our daily lives. We will need special skills to cultivate the capacity to see that "the very
commonness of everyday things harbors the eternal
marvel and silent mystery of God."[14] This mystagogy
would go beyond traditional appeals to some set of
widely accepted religious practices (for example, reading the Bible, celebrating the sacraments, practicing
pious devotions), however important these may be, to
features of ordinary human life that are all too often
overlooked in traditional Christian spirituality. At the
same time, these are the features of ordinary human life
that are most affected when technology flattens out the
rich texture of human relationships.

Let me offer two examples. I attended a dinner party
several years ago at which a guest movingly recounted
a family outing on the Fourth of July. They were celebrating the holiday on the shores of Lake Michigan.
As the sun went down you could see small campfires marking the beach at regular intervals up and
down the long stretch of sand. The campfires cast
shadows of family and friends at play. Then out of

nowhere, fireworks began to shoot off into the night sky. Some were quite beautiful, others were barely visible. Families spontaneously gathered to coordinate this incendiary display and applaud one another's efforts. The dinner guest recalled stepping back to gaze up and down the beach at the dancing flames of campfires and the fireworks illuminating the night sky. She listened to the sounds of waves rhythmically nestling up to the beach and of children playing tag in the sand and felt blessed by the moment. This moment, with its unique composition of a spontaneous experience of human community, the haunting beauty of evening campfires on the beach, and the simple delight of children at play, was for her a graced encounter. Doubtless, on that evening, there were more brilliant exhibitions elsewhere, with commercial pyrotechnic performances set to the sounds of the "1812 Overture." But spectators at those events were just that, spectators. If real celebration took place, it was in spite of, not because of, the technologically sophisticated pyrotechnics they watched. What transpired on the shore of Lake Michigan was a mysterious and blessed coming together of humans to create something wondrous — they were not spectators but participants. And in the communion forged on those shores, there shimmered the grace of God.

Let me offer a second example from my own life. When my wife, Diana, and I had our twin boys, David and Andrew, I was just completing my doctoral studies. In the first few months we were up repeatedly in the night to feed the babies and change their diapers. I recall awakening in the middle of one particular night and being grasped by a profound awareness that has always been somewhat difficult to describe. I realized that right then, changing my son's diaper, I was doing exactly what I was supposed to be doing; I was engaged in an action as vital and fundamental as any I would have in my life. It was a mundane action (a tad unpleasant), part of the daily routine that generally went without significant discussion in our lives. But that basic action of care for our child engaged me in one of life's most vital relationships, a parent nurturing a child. That encounter with my son was a moment of communion and surely a graced moment.

You cannot manipulate such moments. They simply come to us as gift when we live in such a way as to be open to them. The paradox that a technological mindset is incapable of comprehending is that the mundane, the "dead time" of which modern technology and hyperreality would rid us, is often the arena for grace. In her Madeleva Lecture, Kathleen Norris observed:

> It always seems that just when daily life seems most unbearable, stretching out before me like a prison sentence, when I seem most dead inside, reduced to mindlessness, bitter tears or both, that what is inmost breaks forth, and I realize that what had seemed "dead time" was actually a period of gestation.[15]

Norris recalls the spiritual significance of manna, which was given as nourishment for the Israelites and which Jesus himself alluded to in teaching us to ask only for our daily bread. For it was the nature of manna that it was offered daily. While sufficient for one's needs, it could not be stored up.[16] Manna could be received only as "gift," not as commodity. Was there something of this insight in Satan's temptation of Christ to turn stones into bread? Are we not today madly "turning stones into bread" with our often feverish obsession to fill our lives with more and more devices that give us what we want — instantly, without effort, and without engagement? Yet is it not true that grace, our spiritual manna, can only come to us as gift, in our daily waiting and openness to what might emerge from the "insignificant" corners of our world?

I contend that the mystagogical ministry of the church lies precisely in laying bare fundamental connections between, on the one hand, church doctrine and sacramental life, and on the other hand, ordinary events like those that transpired on the beach of Lake Michigan or on my living room floor. In a society in which the goal of much technology is to free us from the mundane burdens and discomforts of diaper changes and improvised fireworks displays, a new commitment to mystagogy is demanded. This mystagogy must affirm the graced dimension of the clumsy, messy, and somewhat improvisational events of ordinary life that become for us "manna in the desert." Returning to Borgmann's call for a reform of the technological shape of our lives, I want to suggest that this reform is in fact a spiritual imperative. It is a call to attend to the patterns of our daily living and to secure, where appropriate, the kinds of focal practices and engagements that can make room for God's coming to be in our life.

At the same time, we must acknowledge the danger that a preoccupation with the discovery of grace in daily life may lead us to overlook the demands that the life of grace places on us. Consequently this new mystagogy must be accompanied by a renewed Christian asceticism appropriate to our times.

A New Asceticism

As we noted in chapter 1, part of both the appeal and the danger of modern technology is that it offers us unlimited consumption of the things we value as a packaged set of experiences with no vulnerability, sacrifice, or inconvenience. Recall our discussion of Disney's Wilderness Lodge. When inconvenience, risk, and vulnerability to the natural elements are strained from one's experience of the "wild," as through cheesecloth, does not the "wild" itself disappear? The technological inventions of Disney are a wonder to behold, but what happens when the Disney genius becomes our guiding ethos, when we look to strain all of our existence of that which is painful, fearful, cumbersome — more importantly, what happens when we come to believe we have the power to do so?

Borgmann contends that the chief cultural concern

of our society "is the craving for the unencumbered enjoyment of all the riches the world and imagination can offer." He further observes that the pleasures of such consumption "require no effort and hence no discipline."[17] What is conspicuously absent, or at least feverishly hidden, in this desire for "unencumbered enjoyment," is the acceptance of what we might call, a bit starkly, the "deathly" dimension of daily life. There is, after all, a shadow side to the recent health craze reflected in the flourishing of gyms, health clubs, and in-home/office exercise equipment. This shadow lies in the not so subtle dependence on the Western obsession with youth that fails to embrace the graced possibilities of aging and the natural diminishment of bodily capacities.

The shape of modern technological living reveals one of the paradoxes of the human spirit. On the one hand, a defining feature of humanity is its capacity for transcendence, its ability to acknowledge both finitude and the presence of limits even as it yearns to go beyond these limits. Cultural anthropologists suggest to us that one of the distinctive features of the *homo sapiens* is its capacity to see death as a limit and, through the use of ritual and myth, to project human existence beyond this limit. On the other hand, what modern technology seems to offer us is less a *transcendence* of limits than the *circumvention* of limits. Human transcendence involves the grappling with our finitude precisely as a way of creatively transcending it. The circumvention of limits requires that one sustain the illusion that finitude can be avoided altogether.

Mark Helprin has captured this paradox in a provocative essay entitled "The Acceleration of Tranquility."[18] Helprin contrasts two "worlds": the projected future of a technology entrepreneur in 2016 and the world of an English diplomat in 1906. The year 2016 offers, he imagines, a world of breathtaking excitement and immediacy. Human beings are miraculously freed from the confines of the office and the traditional workday. The hard-earned wisdom of human history and the entire treasury of human culture are instantly accessible through the computer. This is an intoxicating world filled with immediacy and freedom from almost all forms of constraint. Such mundane skills like handwriting and the ability to perform simple computation are no longer necessary.[19] What Helprin recounts is akin to the world of hyperreality explored by Borgmann. It is a world free of deprivation and, consequently, free of the "compensatory power of the imagination."[20]

The world of Helprin's early twentieth-century English diplomat stands in stark contrast. This individual's life is, by contemporary standards, almost completely circumscribed by limits. Helprin imagines him awaiting an assignment to a new cabinet post while on holiday at Lake Como, Italy. His stay is marked by time spent reading and reflecting. He imagines the graceful silhouette of his wife's body and aches for her presence. He eagerly anticipates a live performance of a piece of music and delights in discerning the author of a just received letter by scrutinizing the penmanship on the envelope.[21] He is able to recall favorite literary passages from memory precisely because he has to — there is no CD-ROM database to which he might refer!

One may of course balk at Helprin's transparent romanticism and rightly point out that the world of 1906 encompassed a good deal more than can be encountered on the idyllic shores of Lake Como. Even Helprin acknowledges that what we must seek is the preservation of a healthy tension between these two worlds. It would be foolish to dismiss the many benefits the world of 2016 offers us. But what that world lacks is "the discipline, values, and clarity of vision that tend to flourish as we grapple with necessity and to disappear when by our ingenuity we float free of it."[22] What distinguished the inhabitants of these two worlds is that the world of 1906 is defined by constraints, deprivations, and necessities that demand the use of memory and imagination. The absence of the giddiness of instant accessibility is compensated for by the perhaps more sublime pleasure of anticipation and contemplation.

Cultural Apathy

What I have described here as the absence of the "deathly" dimension of human experience might be, in fact, a form of cultural apathy. We tend to use the word "apathy" somewhat imprecisely in the sense of a kind of indifference or boredom, a lack of commitment. Apathy certainly includes these elements but the word itself comes from the Greek, *apatheia*, literally, the absence of pathos. Apathy, at its root, refers to the inability to suffer. It is present wherever in our culture there are people so obsessed with avoiding inconvenience, pain, or suffering that they end up avoiding all human relationships that might require risk and vulnerability. This is perhaps the most significant threat that modern technology presents to authentic human existence. In the single-minded pursuit of convenience and disburdenment, the impetus of modern technology unwittingly encourages cultural apathy. The German theologian Dorothee Sölle writes:

> One wonders what will become of a society in which certain forms of suffering are avoided gratuitously, in keeping with middle-class ideals. I have in mind a society in which: a marriage that is perceived as unbearable quickly and smoothly ends in divorce; after divorce no scars remain; relationships between generations are dissolved as quickly as possible, without a struggle, without a trace; periods of mourning are "sensibly" short; with haste the handicapped and sick are removed from the house and the dead from the mind. If changing marriage partners happens as readily as trading in an old car on a new one, then the experiences that one had in the unsuccessful relationship remain unproductive. From suffering nothing is learned and nothing is to be learned.[23]

One consequence of living in a suffering-free state is that we become gradually desensitized to the suffering of others. Sölle observes that increasingly in Western culture

> one learns about the suffering of others only indi-
> rectly — one sees starving children on TV — and
> this kind of relationship to the suffering of others
> is characteristic of our entire perception. We sel-
> dom experience even the suffering and death of
> friends and relatives physically and directly. We
> no longer hear the death rattle and the moaning.
> We no longer touch the warmth and coldness of
> the sick body. The person who seeks this kind of
> freedom from suffering quarantines himself in a
> germ free location where dirt and bacteria cannot
> touch him, where he is by himself, even if this "by
> himself" includes a little family. The desire to re-
> main free from suffering, the retreat into apathy,
> can be a kind of fear of contact. One doesn't want
> to be touched, infected, defiled, drawn in.[24]

This spirit of apathy is directly opposed to the life of communion we described above. For the life of grace and communion is shaped by that most paradoxical of Christian beliefs, the belief that we cannot embrace life unless we accept death.

The Paschal Mystery

At the heart of the Christian faith is the proclamation of the life, death, and resurrection of Jesus Christ — what came to be known in our liturgical tradition as "the paschal mystery." For Christians the cross and resurrection of Christ are not simply significant events punctuating, as it were, the life of Jesus of Nazareth. Rather in the death and resurrection of Christ the distinctive pattern of Christ's manner of living and the distinctive content of his message were fully disclosed. In his ministry and teaching and in his dying and rising Christ revealed to us a pattern of living that offers the possibility of salvation. This life-death-life pattern becomes for us a saving pedagogy. The Gospel of John captures its essence:

> I say to you, unless a grain of wheat falls to the ground and dies, it remains just a grain of wheat; but if it dies, it produces much fruit. Whoever loves his life loses it, and whoever hates his life in this world will preserve it for eternal life. Whoever serves me must follow me, and where I am there also will my servant be. The Father will honor whoever serves me. (John 12:24–26)

In baptism we are drawn into Christ's own death and resurrection and through the life of faith we submit to this saving pedagogy in the imitation of Christ. The working out of our salvation is a matter of making this the characteristic pattern of our lives.

The paschal mystery has a central place in the Christian spiritual tradition. That tradition, in its many forms and moods, is consistently anchored in the sober recognition that we are called by Christ, often against our instincts, to submit to a life of vulnerability in which we risk pain and suffering in a life of love and compassion. We do this knowing that it is only through that willingness to feel pain, to suffer, to know real loss, that we can know delight, gratitude, and the joy of life that the Spirit offers us.

Another term for the pedagogy by which this pattern is internalized is *askesis* or asceticism. In his classic work *Introduction to Spirituality*, Louis Bouyer writes: "Christian asceticism . . . is simply the systematic adaptation of our whole life to this Mystery [the paschal mystery] which should become its soul."[25] By asceticism or *askesis*, then, I mean the concrete discipline by which we enter into the paschal mystery in our daily living.

The martyrs of the early church witnessed to the power of the paschal mystery in the most dramatic form imaginable; through the free offering of their very lives they gave eloquent and sometimes shocking testimony to the power of the cross and resurrection. The witness of the early martyrs eventually gave way to the asceticism of monastic and consecrated religious life. Those who embraced the public profession of the evangelical counsels interpreted the significance of their lives in the light of the *kenosis,* or self-emptying of Christ. To make vows of poverty, chastity, obedience, and sometimes stability, was to freely accept the limitations these vows imposed, but it was also to recognize that through this free embrace would come life eternal. If asceticism often has been associated with unhealthy exercises in self-mortification, the essential truth was nevertheless preserved, namely, that in the Christian life, pain, suffering, emptiness, loneliness, and even boredom — the so called negative characteristics of human existence — must be embraced. Moreover, only through the free embrace of these negativities of human existence could life's graciousness likewise be affirmed.

I believe that the recovery of an authentic, contemporary Christian asceticism is vital if Christianity is to offer an adequate response to the technological shape of daily life. For in a technologically formed world, the "deathly" dimension of human existence is the enemy. As was noted above, much of the seductiveness of technology lies in its promise that we can circumvent limits, not accept them. In contrast, an authentic Christian asceticism affirms that in the plan of God human fulfillment can only come from the free embrace of that which technology and modern consumerism tempt us to circumvent: constraint, loss, and the necessary "friction" of human existence. We dare believe that our lives can in some way be enriched and enlarged by an acceptance of the deathly dimensions of human existence.

What I have tried to offer in this chapter is an account of the character of our God-relatedness and the life of grace that avoids the tendency to separate too facilely the encounter with grace from the "nonreligious" dimensions of our lives. Such a separation ends up, in a typically modern way, "commodifying" grace itself. I believe that this trinitarian vision of God and the life of grace offers a fruitful Christian response to the highly technologized, consumer-oriented society in which we live. The retrieval of this trinitarian account of the life of grace involves, in turn, the recovery of two elements of the Christian tradition, mystagogy and asceticism. Both mystagogy and asceticism are grounded in the basic Christian conviction that grace, blessing, and the possibility of salvation do not come to us in the progressive manipulation of time and maximization of consumption that technology offers us. Rather, they come to us in the conscious attentiveness to the signals of the divine that glimmer in basic human engagements and in the free acceptance of the constraints of time and the "burdens" of human commitment. The true blessings of life can never be simply "ready at hand." Rather, they surprise us in the midst of daily living. This then is the central wisdom of Christianity that needs to be brought to our technological, consumer-driven world: we find human fulfillment precisely when we cease making fulfillment the immediate end of all our actions and instead give ourselves over freely to lives of committed service and love.

In the Christian tradition the cultivation of the work of mystagogy and the disciplined practice of asceticism are never done by isolated individuals. It is in the life of a community of believers that we discover the graced character of daily living, and it is within the life of the community that we are schooled in the distinctive rhythms of paschal living. Mystagogy and asceticism require a community of faith for their full realization. Yet increasingly in North American culture, the pursuit of spirituality is being separated from the life of Christian community. Spiritual seekers do not see church participation as essential to their spiritual quest. We consider this relationship between spirituality and community in the next chapter.

Chapter 3

Toward a Communal Spirituality

In chapter 2 I sketched some of the characteristics of a contemporary spirituality that are appropriate responses to the unique challenges of our technological age. Books on contemporary spirituality are plentiful. Indeed, a new phenomenon emerging on the religious scene is evident in large chain bookstores throughout North America and Western Europe. Alongside the religion section is a new and even larger collection of books on spirituality. The division between spirituality and religion suggests a cultural shift that has been taking place over the last several decades. This shift is reflected in a rather matter of fact comment by Wendy Kaminer in *The New Republic:*

> Spirituality...is simply religion deinstitutionalized and shorn of any exclusionary doctrines....
> You can claim to be a spiritual person without professing loyalty to a particular dogma or even understanding it.[1]

We can find evidence in our culture of a hunger for the transcendent, a longing for some sense of ultimate meaning, but this spiritual quest has become increasingly privatized. In this chapter, I explore the growing split between spirituality and community and suggest some resources within the Christian tradition for healing this split.

Contemporary American Culture and the "Packaging" of Grace

The broad range of contemporary writings that fall under the generic category of spirituality is broad and impossible to treat in detail. Almost all of this literature must be applauded for attempting to respond to the spiritual yearnings of contemporary men and women. More often than not, whether written from within an established Christian tradition or part of the growing body of works on spiritual growth that go beyond traditional religious affiliations, these books successfully explore the desire for a spirituality that speaks to ordinary human experience. Lamentably, appeals to ordinary human experience are often overlooked by the liturgical preachers and religious leaders in mainline churches in general and Roman Catholicism (my own tradition) in particular.

However, much of this literature no longer assumes that the pursuit of the spiritual life requires an affiliation with a formal religious tradition or a Christian community. Wade Clark Roof has suggested that the

source of this more privatized search for transcendence
may lie in the influence of the baby boomer generation,
that demographically significant group of Americans
born between 1946 and 1962. Remarkably diverse,
this generation shares a broad-based suspicion of institutions, secular and religious, that has been fueled
by disenchantment over the Vietnam War, Watergate,
and scandals surrounding public religious figures.[2] An
even more pronounced disassociation of spirituality
and institutional religion by the succeeding generation,
often called "Generation X," has been provocatively
documented by Tom Beaudoin in his book *Virtual
Faith*. Beaudoin observes that while "Xers" often har-
bor a deep cynicism about institutional religion "they
have a widespread regard for paganism" and they
have "a growing enchantment with mysticism." "Xers
take symbols, values, and rituals from various religious
traditions and combine them into their personal 'spirituality.' They see this spirituality as being far removed
from 'religion,' which they frequently equate with a
religious institution."[3]

Mainstream churches themselves have played a role
in the deinstitutionalization of spirituality. For example, Roman Catholicism's doctrinal teaching and/or
pastoral stance toward the divorced and remarried,
gays and lesbians, married couples using artificial con-
traception, and women who feel called to ordained
ministry has led some to seek spiritual sustenance
elsewhere. Additionally, the particular success of American institutional religion in purveying religion as a

commodity — one thinks here not only of the Pat Robertsons and Jerry Falwells but of Norman Vincent Peale in the 1950s — may also have unintentionally loosened the bonds between religious experience and committed membership in a religious tradition.[4]

Whatever the cause, much popular spirituality presents the spiritual journey as an individual quest tailored to the unique contours of one's needs and desires. Individuals are invited to discover the sacred in their midst, but often in ways that reduce spirituality to some "vague, self-referential religiosity." L. Gregory Jones criticizes popular spiritual works that are "shaped by consumer impulses and captive to a therapeutic culture."[5] This literature, he contends, says much about God's presence but little about the absence of God and the need for repentance, conversion, and community. Nor does it address the demands that the spiritual life must make in the way of social and political commitment.

As an illustration, Jones contrasts the works of two popular American writers, Thomas Moore and M. Scott Peck, with a classic Christian spiritual writer, St. Bernard of Clairvaux. For Bernard, as for many of the great spiritual writers of the Christian tradition, the encounter with God was both the fulfillment of the heart's longing and a profoundly sobering recognition of human sinfulness and unworthiness. We discover both the meaning of our being created in the image of God and the humble recognition of our "unlikeness" to God because of sin. The spiritual life for Bernard and others like him is "shaped by both the absence and the presence of God."[6] In the spiritual life we are called to repentance and conversion and to adopt an alternative set of attitudes and practices proper to followers of Christ. These attitudes and practices — some of which are at odds with those in society — are the characteristics that Jones finds lacking in the work of Peck, Moore, and others.

The extent of this privatization of spirituality in our culture may not be so readily apparent because it is often encouraged and supported by churches whose own communitarian sensibilities have diminished. Rather than providing the essential communitarian context for authentic Christian spirituality, many churches today are in danger of becoming what Catherine Albanese calls "boothkeepers in an emporium of transcendence."[7] The church is seen as the "conveyor of a commodity," transcendence, not as a mature Christian community.[8]

Catholicism's strong communitarian tradition has enabled it to resist the privatization of spirituality and the commodification of religious experience, but not completely. In many places the vitality of a parish is measured by the number of programs it runs. Adult education committees select speakers and topics for discussion not by "what the people need to hear" but rather by "what will bring people in." Similarly, the liturgy risks becoming a consumer product evaluated in terms of the quality of music or the number of people involved in the liturgy — the more people involved in the liturgy the better the liturgy.

Some enclaves among the Catholic left have been drawn to the very spiritual literature that Jones pans for its studied avoidance of the traditional categories of sin and repentance. Much of this literature employs an uncritical syncretism that cobbles together scattered bits of wisdom from various religious traditions (for example, the Sufis, Native American spirituality, Eastern religious traditions) and turns this wisdom into a religious commodity, often doing violence to the spiritual coherence of the original traditions in the process. However, as I suggested in the last chapter, the privatized quest for transcendence as a kind of spiritual commodity can also be found on the extreme right of Roman Catholicism — those who advocate the celebration of the Tridentine mass. Too often this return is motivated not by sound liturgical theology but by an uninformed nostalgia. Curiously, many of the strongest advocates for a return to the Tridentine rite are *not* those who have significant memories of the Latin mass but those who project their private yearnings for an experience of the supernatural on a liturgical rite that, in its North American historical context, *was* communal precisely because it was celebrated by ethnically defined immigrant churches who maintained a communal sensibility in other ways. What we find in the retro-liturgies in some traditionalist parishes is not so much a retrieval of the liturgy of the past as a romanticized re-creation. One senses in many of these liturgical traditionalists little more than a superimposition of an individual longing for transcendence on the mere form of a past liturgical rite. In these liturgies everything communal — the sign of peace, welcoming one another at the beginning of the liturgy, baptisms, the catechumenal rites, and ministerial commissionings conducted in the context of the Sunday Eucharist — is muted if not altogether purged from the liturgy. These actions are seen as distractions from the act of worship and one's encounter with Christ in the blessed sacrament.

Of course, one can make the argument that this tendency to commodify religion is not the product of modernity but has always been present in the church. Could we not view the proliferation of non-eucharistic devotional practices in the Middle Ages as a similar kind of commodification? The answer clearly is yes. The difference is that unlike the Middle Ages, when "private devotions" were celebrated in the midst of a much more communitarian cultural sensibility, the modern commodification of religion has few countervailing cultural influences to keep it in check. Premodern communities sustained nonmarket values that limited the social impact of private devotions.[9] In contemporary Western society, however, most social institutions have succumbed to the values of the marketplace and there are few social checks on the technologically driven, consumerist impulse.

In fact, the commodification of religion had already begun in the United States in the nineteenth century. At that time, religious leaders sought to exert influence over the various leisure and entertainment commodities that were being proffered to the public (alcohol and gambling, for example). Operating within the unique parameters of the American separation of church and state, organized religion put forward its own "product" in order to better compete with the many "secular" goods and services that the growing marketplace was offering the consumer. Over time, religion itself became a commodity adapted to the rules of marketing operative in a capitalist culture.[10] Modern technology has rapidly accelerated this process by vastly expanding the realm of religious "choices" and offering them to us in the convenience of our home through mail order pamphlets, religious broadcasting, and now the Internet. Gordon Lathrop voices his concern about the influence of technological consumerism on the churches in this way:

> By appealing to consumerism we may be tacitly saying, here the Roman Catholic sacraments are made available to seeking individuals; here you can "get" the Lutheran word; here the Methodist way; here the Orthodox mystique. Or even here is "church" the way I like it; in the marketplace of religion, I will buy what I need here.[11]

We must avoid sweeping judgments in evaluating this phenomenon. We have to acknowledge that the Enlightenment bequeathed to us much more than consumerism. It also gave us the modern democratic impulse (much of which the church could still incorporate to good benefit), a stress on human rights, and many other positive contributions. Moreover, the demands of Christian evangelization require that we use all means at our disposal to spread the good news of Jesus Christ, including modern media. Our society's expanded capacity to package and sell the goods we desire (including religion) through television and the World Wide Web does not of itself argue against the church's responsible use of these media in service of its mission. However, the notion that these media are value-neutral, as is sometimes suggested, is rather naive.[12] In a technologically driven, capitalist culture, market mechanisms (for example, modern advertising, demographic analyses) are not neutral; they exert their own shape on that which is being marketed. Absent significant counterpressures, the message becomes almost unavoidably commercialized.

All of this suggests that the American religious scene gives evidence of the broader cultural phenomenon we have seen associated with consumerism and modern technology. The goods we value in life become "commodified" whenever they are extracted from the context of human interactions and are produced on demand for the eager consumer. Wed this phenomenon to American individualism and the dictates of a market society and the result is the transformation of religion itself into a commodity.

Authentic Christian discipleship and the life of grace must resist these processes. When religion and the encounter with God become commodities, the ordinary realm of human existence — where God desires to meet us — diminishes in importance. But the life of grace and communion is just that — a life. Grace cannot be neatly extracted, packaged, and sold in ever more appealing ways as a commodity intended to satisfy the spiritual consumer. Christian discipleship demands more than listening to a set of tapes or working on exercises found in a spiritual handbook. It requires immersion in a Christian community, not because that community offers us the spiritual commodities we desire, but because it schools us in practices and attitudes that allow us to recover the sacred dimension of our daily lives.

Toward a Communal Spirituality

The best way to avoid succumbing to the tendencies of our technologically driven consumer culture is to situate the spiritual quest within the context of a commitment to authentic community. However neglected, the resources for cultivating a communal or ecclesial spirituality can be found within the great Christian theological tradition. How we appropriate that tradition will depend largely on how we see the churches relating to the various cultures within which they find themselves.

Christian communities have three basic ways of relating to the larger culture.[13] First, Christian communities can accommodate themselves to the values of the larger culture. As we have seen, this has already taken place in many mainstream American religious traditions, at times with positive results. While Christians could have drawn on resources in their own tradition to challenge the tolerance of slavery, capital punishment, and the denigration of women, for example, in many instances it was the Enlightenment, with its emphasis on human rights and the dignity of the human person, that encouraged the churches to reconsider their positions. Within Roman Catholicism, the Second Vatican Council stressed ways in which the church itself could profit from its engagement with the world (see *Gaudium et spes,* no. 44). But, as we have seen, an uncritical accommodationism has also led to religion and spirituality being held captive to the dictates of consumerism and marketing.

Second, Christian communities can repudiate the larger culture and instead cultivate their own distinctive and generally insular church culture. This is generally referred to as "sectarianism." In its most extreme form sectarianism is found in American Amish communities and some fundamentalist evangelical congregations; in less extreme forms it offers an often vital and bracing evangelical witness to the radical demands of gospel living. Indeed, it is difficult to ignore the quasi-sectarian sensibilities of the churches of the first few centuries, when many Christians viewed themselves as members of a distinctive *ethne* within a world often hostile to Christian purposes and designs.[14] It would be a mistake, however, to assume that simply because the early church found itself struggling to survive in a hostile world, the larger culture in which Christians now live must be viewed everywhere and always as equally hostile to the gospel.

Third, Christian communities can critically engage the larger culture, noting continuities and convergences between church and culture while also identifying gospel values that will lead Christians to criticize the larger culture. This position has been the dominant one within Roman Catholicism, and it is the one that I presume here. This approach recognizes that the Christian community, for all of its distinctive warrants and characteristics, is not resistant to a sociological analysis. If we study any particular Christian community, we easily find similarities to other sociological groupings, clubs, voluntary associations, etc. We import into the church from the larger culture dominant understandings of what constitutes a community. Our symbols, rituals, music, characteristic teaching methods, architecture — all bear the marks of the larger world in which we live. Yet in authentic community these things are also transformed and put to new purposes. As a result, they invite us, not to escape our daily world, but to see it in new ways, illuminated by the light of the gospel.

In the second half of this chapter I would like to explore three views of community, all of which belong to this third category. These, I believe, are particularly helpful for addressing the challenges our age presents to us: the church as the school of discipleship; the church as *koinonia*/communion; and the church as sacrament of God's love.

The Church as the School of Discipleship

The New Testament word for church, *ekklesia*, is drawn from the larger Greek culture in which the word referred to the gathering or assembly of citizens. To see what constituted this gathering in Christianity and made it distinctive, we turn to our English word "church," which is itself adapted from a transliteration of another Greek word, *kyriakon*, meaning "belonging to the Lord." The Christian "gathering" or "assembly" was distinctive in being a gathering of those who belonged to the Lord.[15] Christians shared a belief, a hope grounded in their experience of the risen Lord, that the fullness of life was to be theirs only as they maintained their allegiance to Jesus Christ. This is consonant with a central theme found throughout the gospels, namely, that of discipleship. To be a disciple meant to follow after the master; for Christians, Jesus Christ was the master.

We might say then that the church is both a community or gathering of disciples and at the same time a kind of "school of discipleship." We gather in the full expectation that membership in the Christian community will lay claim to the entirety of our existence. Everything in our lives must be assessed and interpreted within the matrix of beliefs and practices that make this community distinctive. We are "schooled" as disciples when we allow our participation in this community to shed light on every aspect of our existence.

Technology and consumerism can lead to a fragmented existence in which notable spheres of our daily lives are denigrated as insignificant and the mechanisms of the marketplace (including the "religious market-place") tell us the commodities we want and then provide them for us effortlessly. In a culture that is increasingly frenetic and fragmented, learning to follow Christ, to find God in our daily lives and to enter into the pattern of paschal living, is no small feat. So we look to participation in authentic Christian community. Only by hearing God's Word proclaimed (*kerygma*), by common worship and the celebration of the sacraments (*leitourgia*), by experiencing Christian fellowship (*koinonia*), and by engaging in actions of committed service to others (*diakonia*) can we grow as followers of Christ. To reflect on this further I would like to plunder an admittedly overused metaphor for the Christian life, that of the dance.

Consider what is involved in learning to master a particular dance. One of the most popular social activities in Texas during my teenage years was Country and Western dancing — "line dancing," in particular. In line dances like the famous "Cotton-Eyed Joe" a large group of people stand in a line and perform a sequence of coordinated dance steps. I recall my sheepishness and embarrassment as I first tried to grasp the mechanics of Country and Western dancing. There were plenty of bruised shins and at least one bruised ego as I counted the dance steps to myself. Gradually, with the help of formal dance lessons, I overcame my clumsiness and began to internalize the rhythm of the music. I realized then that the real joy of the dancing was to be found, not in the dance studio under the tutelage of instructors, but in the dance hall itself.

I liken involvement in a local community to participation in a dance studio. We enter into the life of the parish or local congregation out of the recognition that, on our own, it is difficult to master the peculiar rhythm of the mystagogical and ascetical existence described in chapter 2. God may be present in our world, but that does not mean that we have learned how to attune ourselves to that presence. Little in our culture prepares us to discover God in the mundane and little encourages us to enter into the pattern of life-death-life that the paschal mystery demands of us. So we come to the church to find "eyes to see and ears to hear." We come in order to discern the demands of the paschal mystery proclaimed in the church's preaching. We learn to master this peculiar rhythm in Bible study and catechetical activities, and we attune ourselves to it both in the work of Christian *diakonia,* or service, and, by means of ritual and symbol, in the celebration of the liturgy. We participate in the life of the local church community, not to take refuge from daily living, but to be schooled in the graced pattern of Christian living and sent out with a renewed sense of divine presence and a renewed recognition of the way of life that the gospel demands of us. In this school of discipleship we discover ourselves in a new way. Our membership in this community becomes a way of life, a life of communion, one that results in a gradual yet far-reaching personal transformation.

The Church as Koinonia/Communion

In chapter 1 we discussed the way in which technological devices, by providing the commodities we desire without the burdens of focal human engagement, can lead us to downplay the value of these basic human activities and engagements. Why go through the trouble of preparing a meal when technology can do the work for me? In chapter 2 we explored a theology of grace and communion that suggests that there is grace and blessing to be discovered in the quality of human engagement itself. This accent on the graced character of human relationship has also been fruitful for reflection on the church as a community constituted relationally.

In the New Testament, *koinonia* is usually translated as "fellowship," "communion," or "participation." The biblical authors employed the word *koinonia* primarily to describe humankind's participation in the divine life of God: "God is faithful, and by him you were called to *fellowship* with his Son, Jesus Christ our Lord" (1 Cor. 1:9). "The grace of our Lord Jesus Christ and the love of God and the *fellowship* of the Holy Spirit be with all of you" (2 Cor. 13:14). Indeed, St. Paul's use of the term *koinonia* suggests an incipient trinitarian theology in which it is through the Son and Spirit that God invites humankind into divine communion. It is in the incarnation, the pinnacle of the economy of salvation, that God makes definitive the divine offer of communion. By our sharing in the death and resurrection of Jesus, celebrated sacramentally in baptism (Rom. 6:3ff.) and in the Eucharist (1 Cor. 10:16–17), we are brought into this divine communion.

St. Paul uses the word *koinonia* to describe the believer's personal participation in the life of God, but this usage does not support any privatized understanding of divine communion. This is evident in St. Paul's description of the church as the body of Christ. Fellowship with God through Jesus comes precisely in and through fellowship in the Christian community. The term *koinonia* expressed the fundamental connection between participation in the life of God and participation in Christian community. Paul's whole ecclesiology presupposed a fundamentally organic view of the church that suggested not just complementarity and diversity within the church but *coexistence*.[16] For Paul, life in Christ meant life in the body of Christ, the church. By baptism into the Christian community one participates in a new reality, one is a new creation. The church was no mere aggregate of individuals and individual believers do not *make* a church. Rather, initiation into the church through faith and baptism *makes* the believer; it introduces the believer into a new mode of existence.

The word *koinonia* also appears in the Acts of the Apostles, where it expresses the communion or fellowship of believers (Acts 2:42). Again, there is a union of the vertical and horizontal dimensions of communion.

In Acts the fundamental ecclesial event is Pentecost, an event that expresses the central role of the Holy Spirit in drawing all believers into spiritual communion. It is the Spirit that transforms a collective of individuals into a living communion of believers.

From a rather different biblical perspective, we find in the Johannine tradition a similar appreciation for the simultaneity of communion with God and communion with one another. "What we have seen and heard we proclaim now to you, so that you too may have *fellowship with us; for our fellowship is with the Father and with his Son, Jesus Christ*" (1 John 1:3–4). For the author of the first Johannine epistle, there is a profound unity between love of God and love for one another:

> God is love, and whoever remains in love remains in God and God in him. . . . If anyone says, "I love God," but hates his brother, he is a liar; for whoever does not love a brother whom he has seen cannot love God whom he has not seen.
>
> (1 John 4:16, 20)

This notion of *koinonia* builds on the trinitarian or relational theism discussed in chapter 2. Love of God and love of others cannot be placed in competition.

In summary, the New Testament offers us a vision of the church as *koinonia,* founded on the Christian conviction that the communion we are offered is a gift of God. It is grace, but it is not a private grace; it is a gift that is realized and nourished in human communion, and preeminently in the communion of believers. Just as communion is an apt expression of the very being of God as life-giving, personal relationality, so communion also names the proper form of all authentic human existence. We are made for communion with God, and no earthly reality, in and of itself, will satisfy. But this spiritual communion with God does not constitute an escape from our daily world. Rather, we come to this communion with God in large part through our embrace of others.

Much like the image of the church as a school of discipleship, the church as *koinonia*/communion presents a vision of Christian community that opens out into our daily, "worldly" existence as Christians. We described the life of communion in chapter 2 as another name for the life of grace. Every authentic embrace of the giftedness of creation, every act of love, is an event of communion and as such it is at the same time an event of grace.[17] Whenever we move out of our own private existence to affirm our world and to enter into "union" with another through actions and relationships that affirm the dignity of others, we are entering into communion with God. As with the "school of discipleship" image, the church as communion also stands in opposition to an overly technologized existence. Communion demands not the consumption of goods but a rich and multifaceted life of human engagement.

It is this life of communion that the church sacramentalizes. In the church, this life of communion, to which all humanity is called, is celebrated in word and sacrament. The church both points to this life of communion and actually effects it through the fulfillment of its mission. Let us turn then to a third image of the church — the church as sacrament.

Church as Sacrament of God's Love

The new mystagogy that was called for in chapter 2 had its inspiration in the theology of grace articulated by that distinguished Catholic theologian Karl Rahner. Rahner's theology reversed a four-century tendency in Catholicism to see grace as something that was "injected" into an otherwise profane world. Rather than following this descending schema in which grace comes as if through a spiritual conduit from Christ through the church and its seven sacraments to the world, Rahner starts with the graced character of the human person in the world. The encounter with God is not relegated to the "practice of religion" but is realized in the very process of being human. In our capacity for wonder, love, hope, and freedom we encounter God. In the experiences of suffering and loneliness, laughter, and play we discover ourselves to be graced. Not surprisingly, Rahner is often called the theologian or mystic of everyday life. He writes:

> The world is permeated by the grace of God....
> The world is constantly and ceaselessly possessed
> by grace from its innermost roots, from the innermost personal center of the spiritual subject....
> Whether the world gives the impression, so far as

our superficial everyday experience is concerned, of being imbued with grace in this way, or whether it constantly seems to give the lie to this state of being permeated by God's grace which it has, this in no sense alters the fact that it is so.[18]

This theology of the abundance and universality of divine grace demands a reinterpretation of sacrament. From within this perspective, a sacrament can no longer be viewed as a "spiritual syringe" that is used to inject grace into graceless people. In fact we must give a certain priority, not to the liturgy and sacraments of the church but to the "liturgy of the world,"[19] for it is the world and not the walls of the church that marks out the primary arena for God's grace. Michael Skelley, in a helpful book on the theology of Karl Rahner, notes a seeming paradox in our experience of God:

> The fact that we continually experience God makes it very difficult for us to be explicitly conscious of experiencing God. We take our experience of the absolute mystery for granted and overlook it, precisely because it is the most pervasive and unavoidable human experience. Our chronic inability to see God in the midst of ordinary daily life is not a confirmation of God's absence but a consequence of God's radical presence.... The one experience of life that should, theoretically, be the most apparent to us is in fact the most hidden.[20]

The hiddenness of God's presence in the daily lives of men and women demands a visible sign which reveals the reality of that which is experienced. For Rahner it was the task of the church to "point ever anew to this basic experience of God."[21]

One of the significant revolutions in Catholic thinking that occurred in this century was the growing recognition of a number of scholars that while it was true that the church possessed certain sacraments — effective signs of God's grace — it was also true that the church was itself an effective sign of God's redemptive love. The church is a visible, communal sign of God's redemptive love for humanity. This notion must be developed further.

If the grace encountered in the midst of daily life is likely to go without note, the grace encountered in the church is manifested more explicitly through religious symbols and ecclesial actions. That which is hidden is, under God's subtle direction, ceaselessly struggling to become visible and concrete. Participation in the life of the church becomes a means of opening our eyes to that divine presence in the world. In the reconciling ministry of the church, for example, the grace of the sacraments disposes us to discover the ways in which God invites us to reconciliation in our homes, workplaces, and civic communities. Far from presenting the church as an oasis of grace, the sacramentality of the church breaks open our daily life and offers us a new vision of its graced character. We might say that the ministry of the church serves to name, in ritual and symbol, the grace that we experience in daily life.[22] At the same time, the life of the church both expands and deepens our experience of that grace. In the witness of holy men and women, the proclamation of Scripture, the celebration of the liturgy and sacraments, and the work of Christian service, we find in concrete and visible form that which has lain hidden in the routine of daily living. In this discovery, the encounter with God takes on a greater texture and depth. Faithful participation in the life of the church should make of us all "mystagogues," believers attuned to the mysterious play of God in our lives.

The church also calls us to be modern ascetics, Christians schooled in the paschal patterns of God's redemptive love. Indeed, as a sign of God's redemptive love, the church speaks a prophetic word to all that stands in opposition to the paschal rhythm of life-death-life.[23] Here the sacramentality of the church involves more than a mystagogy, a naming of the mysterious presence of God in our lives. In the accomplishment of its mission the church also reveals the peculiar *shape* of divine love. For if the love of God was revealed in Jesus Christ as a love realized in the pattern of dying and rising, then the church as the sacrament of this redemptive love becomes the place in which we are invited to adopt this paschal rhythm as the necessary rhythm of the life of grace. This is evident in that very ritual by which Christians are initiated into community, baptism. The twofold imagery of ancient baptisteries as both womb and tomb reinforced the paschal pattern of life to death to new life that was to become, for the neo-phytes, the vital pattern by which they were to shape their lives.

Focal Practices of the Christian Community

This Christian community that schools us in the ways of discipleship, invites us into *koinonia* with God and others, and stands, in spite of its transparent broken-ness, as a sacrament of God's redemptive love — this church calls us to a unique way of life through the telling of the Christian story in word and symbol and through our participation in a distinctive set of ecclesial activities or practices appropriate to those who "be-long to the Lord." Here we can return fruitfully to Borgmann's concept of "focal practices."

Recall Borgmann's warning that the technological device, unlike the focal thing, diminishes our capac-ity for real human engagement with our world and the enjoyment of the goods that are by-products of that engagement. What we need, he insists, is the reinvigo-ration of our lives with the skill of true celebration. For real human celebration, he reminds us, involves both discipline and grace. In our modern technolog-ical world, both are at risk. The demands of human discipline have been replaced by machinery and devices that require no craft and little schooling for their main-tenance. Grace, on the other hand, has been replaced by a cheap gratification offered by commodities that do not call us forth into "the land of the living" but encourage the passivity of the consumer.[24] We need to make a conscious effort to preserve those vital focal practices that bring grace and blessing into our lives. Norman Maclean captures the spiritual significance of such focal practices in his account of fly fishing. In his novel *A River Runs through It,* Maclean reflects on the way in which grace and blessing come to us, not as some instantly accessible commodity but in the exercise and discipline of focal practice, in this case the practice of fly fishing. His account is worth quoting at length.

> In our family, there was no clear line between religion and fly fishing. We lived at the junction of great trout rivers in western Montana, and our father was a Presbyterian minister and a fly fisherman who tied his own flies and taught others. . . . In a typical week of our childhood Paul and I probably received as many hours of instruction in fly fishing as we did in all other spiritual matters. After my brother and I became good fishermen, we realized that our father was not a great fly caster, but he was accurate and stylish and wore a glove on his casting hand. As he buttoned his glove in preparation to giving us a lesson, he would say, "It is an art that is performed on a four-count rhythm between ten and two o'clock."
>
> As a Scot and a Presbyterian, my father believed that man by nature was a mess and had fallen from an original state of grace. Somehow, I early developed the notion that he had done this

by falling from a tree. As for my father, I never knew whether he believed God was a mathematician but he certainly believed God could count and that only by picking up God's rhythms were we able to regain power and beauty. Unlike many Presbyterians, he often used the word "beautiful."

My brother and I would have preferred to start learning how to fish by going out and catching a few, omitting entirely anything difficult or technical in the way of preparation that would take away from the fun. But it wasn't by way of fun that we were introduced to our father's art. If our father had had his say, nobody who did not know how to fish would be allowed to disgrace a fish by catching him.

Until man is redeemed he will always take a fly rod too far back, just as natural man always overswings with an ax or golf club and loses all his power somewhere in the air; only with a rod it's worse, because the fly often comes so far back it gets caught behind in a bush or rock....

Then, since it is natural for man to try to attain power without recovering grace, he whips the line back and forth making it whistle each way, and sometimes even snapping off the fly from the leader, but the power that was going to transport the little fly across the river somehow gets diverted into building a bird's nest of line, leader, and fly that falls out of the air into the water about ten feet in front of the fisherman....

> Power comes not from power everywhere, but
> from knowing where to put it on. "Remember,"
> as my father kept saying, "it is an art that is per-
> formed on a four-count rhythm between ten and
> two o'clock."
>
> My father was very sure about certain mat-
> ters pertaining to the universe. To him, all good
> things — trout as well as eternal salvation — come
> by grace and grace comes by art and art does not
> come easy.[25]

Maclean wonderfully depicts the central characteristics of a "leisure" activity as a focal practice. Fly fishing
demands discipline and attentiveness to the moment. It
incorporates skills that can be acquired only through
an interpersonal, tutelary relationship. It has clear and
even daunting standards of excellence. It invites the participant into a world of engagement with nature that,
in its very richness, introduces an element of unpre-
dictability and openness that is vital to the experience
of fishing. The success of a fishing excursion depends
on factors largely outside of the fisherman's control:
weather, river flow, etc. Indeed, a good deal of the joy
of fishing comes from successfully adapting to these
variables. Clearly the joys of fly fishing, for Maclean,
involve much more than the acquisition of fresh fish!
"Grace" and "salvation" come "by art and art does
not come easy."

A central contention of this volume is that the Christian community itself possesses a distinctive set of such

"focal" practices. These practices call us into transformative patterns of human engagement. They effect our conversion by inviting us into the life-death-life pattern of paschal living and they help us recover "the eyes to see and ears to hear" God in the sacred domain of daily living. These "sacred practices," when engaged fully and richly, have the capacity to reorient our daily lives.[26] Among these "sacred practices" we might include baptismal initiation, the *lectio divina* (or spiritual reading of Scripture), and the many popular devotions that often emerge out of the particular interplay of faith and culture. Among the many practices that Christians engage in, we will consider but two, the work of *diakonia,* or Christian service to others, and the celebration of the liturgy of the church (discussed in the next chapter).

The ministry of *diakonia* can take many forms, but all of its manifestations share a concern for attending to the needs of others. And yet, what is distinctive about Christian *diakonia* is that service to others is not undertaken merely for the sake of the other, but also because of the conversion it effects in the one who serves. The gospel certainly demands that we exercise compassion for others and seek to realize a more just world in all that we do as a preparation for the coming of God's reign. Still, the call to justice does not exhaust the Christian call to service. We do not give service to others solely because it will improve the lives of those we serve. This may seem odd, but upon reflection we can see the importance of this insight. If our exercise of service were to focus exclusively on the improvement of the welfare of others, this *diakonia* could fall prey to the calculus of cost-benefit analysis in which we only give service when we can foresee the fruitfulness, the effectiveness of our giving. Yet many great figures in the Christian tradition — from St. Francis of Assisi to Mother Teresa and Dorothy Day, along with countless thousands who minister to the homeless, abandoned, and dying — all remind us that service to others carries within it its own logic, the logic of God's self-gift, the paschal mystery. Stephen Webb, in his fine book *The Gifting God*, develops the distinctive spiritual logic at work here:

> We do not give in order to receive for ourselves but in order to give something back to God who gives. Our giving is not governed by the logic of compensation and return but by the desire to follow the essential dynamic of all gifts, which is to return them to their origin, in God, by giving them to others. By receiving our gifts, God solicits our giving even when that giving does not seem to make a difference, or when it seems too difficult to give.... We do not have to choose between giving to God and giving to others; by giving to others, we are participating in the momentum of God's giving, which multiplies and disperses gifts even as they are directed to the one Giver.[27]

What we have here is a spiritual theology of gift-giving that, as we shall see in the next chapter, unites

diakonia to Christian liturgy. Webb creates a neologism, *gifting,* to highlight the reality that, from a
theological perspective, the act of giving to others pre-
supposes that we have already been *gifted* by God.
"Gifting is the unreserved act in which we are most
truly ourselves, supported and sustained in the dynamic becoming of God, finding ourselves by losing
ourselves in the other." Christian service, then, is not
to be confused with social work, inasmuch as *diakonia*
is grounded in the theology of the "gifting God" whose
own self-gift "precedes and empowers our giving."[28]

I have suggested in this chapter a way of consider-
ing the relationship between a spirituality of everyday
life and participation in the life of the church. As both
community of discipleship and sacrament, the life of the
church has much to contribute to a spirituality of the
everyday. We are invited to find God in the midst of our
daily lives, yet it is the distinctive practices that constitute the Christian community that transform us, draw
us into the life of communion, and give us "the eyes to
see" the possibilities for authentic discipleship in our
world. As Christians we believe that a life formed by
the distinctive practices and values of the church gives
us the best chance of resisting both the commodification and the privatization of grace encouraged by our
technological, consumerist culture. Contemporary spirituality may need to be "deinstitutionalized," but its
flourishing depends upon the Christian's participation
in a living community of faith.

Chapter 4

Liturgy of the Church, Liturgy of the World

If the church is itself a sacrament of God's redemptive love for us, then the celebration of the Christian liturgy is the privileged manifestation of God's love in ritual and symbol. In the celebration of the Christian liturgy the people of God gather together and unite themselves with Christ in his paschal offering. In doing so, the people of God offer corporate *eucharistia*, praise and thanksgiving to God in union with Christ by the power of the Spirit. As such, the liturgy is clearly an event of grace, an encounter with God in the proclamation of the Word, in the breaking of the bread and the sharing of the cup. Yet, though an event of grace, we must resist seeing the liturgy as a *conduit* of grace, drawing upon some supernatural reservoir that makes available to the world that which is otherwise lacking. For almost four hundred years Roman Catholicism suffered from a theology of sacramental grace that viewed the church as a sacramental grace-dispenser that "injected" grace into a grace-less world.

In this chapter I want to reflect on the place of
the liturgy in the Christian life in a way that avoids
the "ecclesial grace-dispenser" model and explains instead how our participation in the liturgy involves us
in a transformative focal practice. By that I mean that
our very participation in the liturgy is the ritual enact-
ment of a set of Christian dispositions and values that
challenges the basic characteristics of our technological
culture.

The Liturgy is the Celebration
of the Christian Life

In chapter 2 I sketched out an account of trinitarian or
relational theism and a theology of grace that rejects
any attempt to place our relationship with God and the
concerns of our daily lives in competition. I suggested
that we discover the life of grace in the daily invitation to communion with others and with the world
itself. But does not this theology of grace render super-
fluous "institutional religion"? In chapter 3 I tried to
show why a theology that affirms the graced dimension
of ordinary life does not negate the value and indeed
importance of participation in a Christian community.
Among the many distinctive practices of the Christian
community, none is more central than the celebration
of the liturgy. I would now like to consider how the
celebration of the liturgy in the life of the church can
challenge and transform our experience of daily life.

The Second Vatican Council wrote that the liturgy is

"the summit toward which the activity of the church is directed; it is also the source from which all its power flows" (*Sancrosanctum Concilium,* no. 10); some were critical of this statement's implicit devaluation of the nonliturgical spheres of Christian living. Surely the mission of the church to transform the world is of equal importance? Yet this criticism fails to grasp the true intention of this passage. We must recall that at its root the liturgy is a *celebration* of the Christian faith. This is quite different from saying that the liturgy is the *entirety* of the Christian faith or even the unique *preserve* of the Christian faith. Rather, it is in the liturgy that we enact in ritual and symbol the daily life of communion. Thus all of Christian life will be *related* to the liturgy inasmuch as the liturgy is the ritualized celebration of what transpires in our lives, under the work of God's grace, daily.

It is ironic that the so-called "high churches" — Roman Catholicism, Orthodoxy, and the various Anglican communions — are referred to in this way because they are thought to have a strong sense of "the sacred" as it is encountered in ritual and symbol. I say ironic, because I believe that the true nature of the liturgy does not lie in its being a "sacred act of worship" radically distinct from our ordinary human activities.[1] Rather, in the liturgy we recall the entrance of God in history. God incarnate abides with us in the most insignificant and mundane, even homely, circumstances. In Jesus Christ God embraced all of creation as a suitable abode for the divine.

The Bible reports to us the many signs and wonders that Jesus performed, the great teachings he left us, and the redemptive power of his suffering, death, and resurrection. But it is easy to forget that Jesus of Nazareth apparently lived for some thirty years as something of a peasant or a craftsman in a small town. He practiced a trade and, following the death of his father, took care of a family. We have no record of his performing miracles during this time. There are no indications of any adolescent sermons on the mount save for an account (of questionable historicity) of a brief foray in the temple at the age of twelve. When, later in his public ministry, Jesus returns to Nazareth, his reception there suggests that nothing in his childhood prepared the residents of Nazareth for who he would become. Jesus of Nazareth, the Word Incarnate, lived most of his earthly existence practicing a trade and taking care of a family! In short, the incarnation affirms that God is to be discovered in a world filled with mundane daily tasks for which few are canonized: the world of family and work, the world of daily labor, meal preparation, and household chores. He took all that is ordinary and, to our modern eyes, boring and without value, and he blessed it and made it holy.

The incarnation represents the transcendence of any division between the sacred and the secular or profane. Jesus himself said that the only profane "realities" were those that issued from human sin, "nothing that enters one from the outside can defile that person; but the things that come out from within are what defile" (see Mark 7:15). With the coming of Christ the inner transformation of the whole world was begun.

This transformation of all profane existence into the dwelling place of God is taken up in the liturgy. The Christian liturgy celebrates the paschal mystery, the life, death, and resurrection of Jesus Christ, as the unique pattern by which all enter into spiritual communion. In the liturgy we unite ourselves with Christ who gives himself "for the life of the world" in such a way that the liturgy becomes itself a ritual pedagogy that schools us in the life of communion. The great Orthodox theologian Alexander Schmemann wrote that the liturgy "is not an escape from the world, rather it is the arrival at a vantage point from which we can see more deeply into the reality of the world."[2] Consequently, as another Orthodox theologian put it, we are sent forth from the Eucharist to celebrate "the liturgy after the liturgy."[3] Karl Rahner had much the same thing in mind when he wrote of the "liturgy of the world."[4] This liturgy is nothing less than the transformation of the world as the arena in which we might enter into communion with one another and all creation as a sacrament of God's presence. Yet it is also this liturgy of the world that is being undermined by certain aspects of our technological society. When technology devalues human engagement, commodifies human goods, eliminates all forms of human friction, and circumvents all experiences of human limitation, our capacity to enter into this liturgy of the world is diminished. This diminishment heightens our need for the liturgy of the church as the "sacred place," properly understood, in which we discover the "holy ground" that is our daily life.

"Holy Things for Holy People"

In the Eastern liturgy, immediately before the fraction, the deacon elevates the eucharistic gifts and proclaims: "Holy things for holy people." Indeed the liturgy is focused on "holy things": bread, wine, water, oil. As Gordon Lathrop has demonstrated so eloquently, the liturgy is very much concerned with the juxtaposition of these "holy things":

> The primary theology of the liturgy . . . begins with things, with people gathered around certain central things, and these things, by their juxtapositions, speaking truly of God and suggesting a meaning for all things.[5]

What is it that makes these "things" holy? In a sense we can speak of the "natural" holiness of the objects of the liturgy. For example, bread is holy not just in view of its use in the liturgy but because it represents basic human sustenance.[6] And yet, while it is important for their effective functioning as ritual symbols that bread and cup resemble the bread and cup of daily life, Christian liturgical practice has generally resisted presenting them in the full ordinariness of their daily usage. This has been taken to an extreme: flat, tasteless hosts resemble cardboard more than bread and gaudy chalices have no connection to the cups we use for drinking.

Nevertheless, we seem to recognize the need for a kind of "otherness" that should characterize the holy things of the liturgy.[7] Without losing their vital connection to daily life, the materials that will be put to ritual use take forms that distinguish them from their more utilitarian purposes. The chalice becomes itself a fine work of art cast by a master metal-worker. The bread is both familiar and yet takes a form that distinguishes it from table bread. What results is a "symbolic distancing" in which our engagement with these sacred objects draws us out of our ordinary world. The eucharistic banquet is reminiscent of a meal, yet it is celebrated with a sufficient formality to remind us of the eschatological banquet that is not yet ours to celebrate in its fullness. In the celebration of the Eucharist we feel a certain tension between what is and what is to come. In the celebration of this meal, with bread that is not quite like ordinary bread, with a chalice that is no mere dinner tumbler but the cup of eternal salvation, we are drawn into a different "place," as it were. The juxtaposing of the familiar with the unfamiliar creates a sense of disorientation and this disorientation allows us to confront anew, as from the outside, precisely the character of our everyday world that otherwise, by its very ordinariness, might escape examination. This is the meaning of the "sacred" from an anthropological point of view — being set apart, not as an escape but in order to see one's life in a new way. In ritual action, conventional expectations are turned on their head and the sense that "things are different" creates the space in which real transformation or conversion can happen.[8] As Nathan Mitchell once observed, "At its deepest root, Christian liturgy is *parable* — a provocative assault on our customary way of viewing life, world, and others."[9]

"Holy Things" Engender Christian Focal Practices

These "holy things" are not mere objects for adoration; they are also "objects put to use." Consequently, the holy things of the liturgy call for a set of ritual practices. Vatican II's Constitution on the Sacred Liturgy holds that "the faithful should be led to take that full, conscious, and active part in liturgical celebrations *which is demanded by the very nature of the liturgy*" (no. 14, emphasis added). The council suggests, in this quite remarkable passage, that participation in the liturgy by the whole community is not an aesthetic nicety but rather is essential to the doing of the rite itself. Holy things demand human engagement; they must be put to use. The power and meaning of these things is inseparable from the ritual practices they demand.

I contend that the celebration of the liturgy is the paradigmatic focal practice of the Christian life. As focal practice, liturgical rituals demand manifold engagement: in liturgy we are drawn into a richly variegated encounter with the worship environment (the actual shape or architecture, sights and sounds of the worship space), the presence of the assembly, our own bodiliness in the form of ritual postures and gestures (standing or kneeling, sign of the cross, kiss of peace), and the "holy things" at the heart of the ritual action (water, oil, bread, wine). Liturgical ritual, like other focal practices (recall Maclean's description of fly fishing), demands significant preparation and the transmission of a discrete set of skills for those who would exercise the various forms of liturgical ministry. Just as the goods procured through focal practices are inseparable from the practices themselves, so too we hold that the grace of sacramental action cannot be reduced to some supernatural "stuff" isolated from the ritual action of ministers and community.

As a constellation of holy (focal) things and ritual (focal) practices, the liturgy has the power to subvert the device paradigm. Unlike the technological device, the liturgy *does* call attention to itself; it *does* create "burdens"; it *does* call for manifold engagement; it *does* demand a set of skills and disciplines. As the root meaning of the Greek word *leitourgia*, suggests, liturgy is the "work of the people." The celebration of the liturgy demands our engagement in ritual actions that shape us precisely through our participation in them. Moreover, we must resist the temptation to think that these ritual practices are simply expressions of prior convictions and commitments originating in some kind of cognitive form. As Theodore Jennings reminds us, there is a distinctive kind of "ritual knowledge" that is inseparable from these distinctive bodily engagements.

Ritual knowledge is gained through a bodily action which alters the world or the place of the

> ritual participant in the world.... Ritual knowl-
> edge is gained in and through the body.... It is
> not so much that the mind "embodies" itself in
> ritual action, but rather that the body "minds"
> itself or attends through itself in ritual action.
> When engaged in ritual action (let us take the
> performance of the Eucharist and the ritual-like
> activity of disco dancing as disparate examples), I
> do not first think through the appropriate action
> and then "perform" it. Rather it is more like this:
> My hand "discovers" the fitting gesture (or my
> feet the fitting step) which I may then "cerebrally"
> *re*-cognize as appropriate or right.[10]

This is not a knowledge that is first grasped intel-
lectually and then translated into action. This is a
knowledge grasped only in the doing. With striking
resonances to Borgmann, Jennings observes that this
ritual knowledge

> is gained not through detachment but through en-
> gagement — an engagement that does not leave
> things as they are but which alters and trans-
> forms them.... The performance of the ritual,
> then, teaches one not only how to conduct the
> ritual itself, but how to conduct oneself outside
> the ritual space — in the world epitomized by
> or founded or renewed in and through the ritual
> itself.[11]

In this sense we might speak of the pedagogical character of ritual. Consider the way liturgical ritual can
affect our experience of time.[12]

The liturgical ritual is not concerned with the mastery of time but rather with allowing the participants
to align themselves, by means of ritual, to "God's
rhythms." In short, we learn how to tell "God's time."
This pedagogy is disclosed not only in the celebration of
each Eucharist itself, but in the liturgy of the hours and
the pattern of the whole liturgical calendar. The celebration of the liturgy and the liturgical year demand
nothing less than the transformation of time itself.[13]

This aspect of Christian liturgy is particularly important for a culture like ours that is so obsessed with the
mastery of time. Even actively committed Christians
tend to see the issue of time as one of finding a place
for "religious time" in their busy lives. They will hero-
ically seek to carve out a place for Sunday Eucharist,
children's catechesis, and perhaps a weeknight parish
meeting of one kind or another. But as Regis Duffy has
noted, "There is always a temptation to think of religious time as personal time set aside for worship and
'good works' and to forget the invitation to change radically our perspective on the larger Christian purposes
of time."[14] The liturgy offers us the chance to "heal"
our conception of time so driven by technological mastery. When Vatican II spoke of the "sanctification of
time" with respect to the liturgy of hours (the modern
form of which is derived from prayer at set times during the day common to monastic life) it did not mean

that secular time is rendered sacred through this prayer form. Rather, Stanislaus Campbell contends, the phrase meant that the celebration of the liturgy of the hours exhibits "at certain times of the day what the quality of all times should be, that is, an experience of time which is sacramental or revelatory of the mystery of Christ and a means of union with God in him."[15]

I believe that the cultivation of the liturgy as a Christian focal practice can help us detect the erosion of the kind of focal practices in our daily lives that provide occasions for grace. In the whole pattern of the liturgy, in its overall shape, we are formed by the paschal pattern of life-death-life that was revealed to us by Christ in his life and teaching as the only way to human fulfillment.[16] It will be helpful to consider a bit more concretely how the liturgy can effect this kind of transformation.

Liturgy of the Church, Liturgy of the World

When we enter into the liturgy, our engagement with the liturgical symbols and rituals, themselves drawn from daily life, break open our daily lives and reveal both the hidden possibilities for communion that can be found there and the obstacles that impede the life of communion. This is what Mitchell calls "ritual engagement." The ritual action changes us. It reconfigures the way we view our world, giving us "new eyes to see." Mitchell observes that "we become hospitable, for instance, not by analyzing hospitality but by greeting guests, offering them the kiss of peace, washing their feet, serving them food, adoring Christ's presence in them."[17] Let us consider two concrete aspects of the liturgy that can help reshape the way we view our daily lives: eucharistic feasting, and our capacity for gift giving and receiving.

Eucharistic Feasting

In his thoughtful reflections on celebrating the Eucharist in "diet America," Patrick McCormick notes an alarming inability to feast in an American culture that knows only dieting and bingeing. What do we do with studies that tell us that "80 to 85 percent of American women experience eating disorders at some point in their lives" and "fifty million Americans are currently dieting to lose weight"?[18] Lost is the sensual pleasure of a good meal. The symbolic power of feasting is eclipsed in a culture that thinks of food either in terms of nutrition, hence the uniquely American obsession with dieting, or efficiency, reflected in the American invention of fast food.

Of all the goods that have been "commodified" by technology none has been subjected to greater commodification than food itself. The shift from subsistence farming and ranching to modern agribusiness means that while supermarkets always have a plentiful supply of food, we have lost our sense of the remote origins of our food. We no longer know who planted and harvested the food we purchase. Nor are we connected to even the proximate origins of our food. As we noted in chapter 1, the home cooked meal in which the household cook was the proximate originator of the meal we consume has been replaced by the prepackaged microwave meal. Having lost its capacity to connect us with our larger world, food has become a mere commodity to be consumed rather than enjoyed.

The very abundance of food similarly makes it almost impossible for us to know anything about true fasting. To fast is to voluntarily enter into the experience of hunger, both to stimulate our hunger for God and to stand in solidarity with those who hunger daily. But dieting is not fasting. Dieting is an extension of the American love/hate relationship with our own bodies.[19] It encourages us to think of food in an increasingly narcissistic fashion — as something related to personal appearance and personal health. These are not evils in themselves, but they are values strikingly unrelated to the larger world of human relationships (except for the relationship with those whose opinion of our appearance matters to us). Our cultural obsession with dieting fits well within the technological shape of daily living. This is readily apparent when we recognize that dieting is often concerned with gaining control over our very mortality. "Increasingly we expect our diets to prevent illness, retard aging, and conquer death itself."[20] Dieting sees food as the enemy to be conquered in an attempt to control our fate.

And so we come to the liturgy to transform the pattern of bingeing and dieting into that of feasting and fasting. In the liturgy we are reminded that the meal we celebrate has its roots in the earth and in the larger world of human relationships. Before we come to the table we confess our sins and offer Christ's peace to one another. We pray for one another and offer alms for the poor. Throughout the liturgy we recall our connections with those who are not physically gathered around the table: the communion of saints, the universal church, all people of good will. The Eucharist is less about food consumed than it is a meal shared, and the food to be shared at this meal is no mere commodity. For the bread we break is that which "earth has given and human hands have made" and the wine we share is "fruit of the vine and work of human hands."

This feast is no casual affair. We dress up in "Sunday clothes" and vestments, we break out the musical instruments and song books, we carefully prepare a table with flowers and candles and banners because this is a feast we are celebrating and not a "power lunch." Yet this feast we celebrate is no exclusive affair. As a community of disciples we are called to imitate Christ's scandalously inclusive table fellowship in which unconditional hospitality was proffered to all who would come. As Fr. Bob Hovda once observed so eloquently, the eucharistic liturgy is an exercise in "contradiction":

> Where else in our society are food and drink broken and poured out so that everybody shares and shares alike, and all are thereby divinized alike? Where else do economic czars and beggars get the same treatment? Where else are we all

addressed with the proclamation of a word we
believe to be God's, not ours, and before which
we all stand equal? Where else are we all sprin-
kled and bowed to and incensed and touched and
kissed and treated like *somebody* — all in the same
way? This is playing the reign of God. This is an
alternative in contradiction, in sharp distinction,
to our status quo. This classless society is the way
things ought to be.[21]

We come to the eucharistic feast to "play the reign of
God." In ritual and symbol we "act as if" this were
a world already governed by God's shalom. And we
hope that this eucharistic feasting in the liturgy of the
church might lead us to a like feasting in the liturgy of
the world. We hope that it will help us rediscover the
transformative power of even our daily meals in the
sharing of food with our families and friends, but, perhaps more importantly, with our enemies and strangers
as well. McCormick writes:

> In the end, then, an authentic celebration of the
> Eucharist awakens us to our deepest ties to God,
> creation, and our neighbors, uncovers and cele-
> brates the ways we are nurtured by and dependent
> upon all three of these. Even more, it makes us
> conscious of our personal, social and ecological
> sinfulness, of the ways in which we fail to attend
> to or treat justly those who have brought us our
> food, who have kept us alive. For in the Eucharist

we are acknowledging and celebrating our ties to the earth and all the life forms that generate and recycle food to satisfy our hungers. We are confessing our dependence upon and obligations to those who labor — often under grievously unjust conditions — to bring us our "daily bread." And we are recalling our intimate connection to those who hunger for food on a planet where too few have too much.[22]

The Eucharist, then, becomes a prophetic action of the church that speaks to a culture that is fast losing its capacity to fast or to feast. This capacity is itself rooted in our ability to enter into a world of gifts: gifts received, gifts given, and gifts shared.

Liturgy and Our Capacity for Gift Giving and Receiving

The liturgy, when faithfully enacted, calls for the recovery of a way of living, an attentiveness to the unpredictable eruptions of grace and blessing in the midst of daily life that are too often eclipsed and defaced by sin. Here liturgical celebration may be considered fruitfully from another perspective, the understanding of sacramental grace as "gift."[23]

The grace we receive in the celebration of the sacraments, to be truly a *gift* of grace, cannot be commodified. It cannot be something subject to our manipulation and control. Consider for a moment the different ways in which we conceive of gifts, or more accurately, gift giving and receiving, in our modern culture. On the one hand, there are social conventions regarding the exchange of gifts at birthdays, weddings, graduations, and major holidays. Most of us operate within certain unwritten yet tacitly accepted expectations regarding the number and appropriate price range of gifts. These expectations are generally specific to our particular ethnic background, family customs, age, and social class. In our household, with so many of our children being invited to the birthday parties of their peers, my wife has taken to stockpiling appropriate gift items such as children's books and age-appropriate games. Though we are embarrassed to admit it, the value of the gifts frequently figures in significantly. Where we anticipate an exchange of gifts, as would be the case at Christmas among friends or members of the family, there may be a certain anxiety about being part of an inequitable exchange. What if our best friends spend lavishly on our children while our own gifts are more modest? Such anxiety can seldom be brought out into the open, but it does govern many of these kinds of exchanges.

On the other hand, we may also enter into an altogether different kind of gift exchange. I am thinking now of the kind of gift I receive from my children when they run up and embrace me after I have returned from a trip; the wholly unexpected gift of forgiveness my wife has offered me time and again in our marriage; the gift a friend offered to Diana and me at our wedding when he performed a piece of music written for the occasion; the miraculous gift of new life witnessed in a birthing room; the gift Beethoven left us all in the exhilarating chorus of the fourth movement of his ninth symphony; the gift great athletes from Pele to Michael Jordan to Nolan Ryan to Nadia Comenici have given to fans throughout the world through their athletic artistry and competitive spirit. As Louis-Marie Chauvet observes, such gifts are both *gracious* and *gratuitous*.[24] They are *gracious* because we cannot quantify their value. The worth of a child's homemade Father's Day card cannot be measured according to any objective scale of value, precisely because it represents a break from the world of commerce and an entrance into the world of *self*-gift. At the same time, such gifts are also *gratuitous* because they are unmerited. Yet even gifts such as these, as gracious and gratuitous as they may be, call for a kind of reciprocation, if only in the expression of gratitude or delight. The difference, of course, is that in this exchange of gifts there are no conventions demanding a rough equivalency precisely because such gifts transcend that kind of calculation. Nevertheless, without the fulfillment of the obligation of the return-gift, however incommensurable it may be, there can be no true communion. Indeed, it is the way in which this exchange transcends valuation that moves it beyond the realm of commerce and social convention into the realm of grace and communion.

This second kind of gift exchange lies at the heart of the celebration of the liturgy. As we submit ourselves to its paschal rhythms and abandon our hard-won mastery of time and our tendency to turn all things into commodities subject to our manipulation and control, we open ourselves up to the possibility of divine gift as God comes to us in Christ by the power of the Spirit and invites us to offer our humble return gift of praise and worship and the sacrifice of our lives.

Consider the character of the act of praise itself. As with the dynamic of gift-giving discussed in relation to *diakonia* in chapter 3, praise operates according to the peculiar logic of overflow, of giving without measure, "for praise perfects perfection."[25] This explains the power of "speaking in tongues" for those of a more charismatic spirituality. Our desire to praise overruns our reason and so we give our tongues, moved by the Spirit, free reign. What occurs in our praise of God is at least analogous to our praise of other persons. When I praise others or express my love for them I might think that this expression or act of praise serves as mere gloss adding something additional to the relationship. But in fact this is not the case. My love for my wife cannot be separated so easily from my *expression* of my love to her in words and affectionate gestures. The actual expression of love doesn't just add something to a preexisting relationship; it actually constitutes a new relationship. And so with God the act of giving praise itself places us in a new relationship with God. This movement to give praise and thanksgiving is itself initiated by the Spirit who unites us with Jesus, the one who first taught us to pray to God. We offer such "return gifts," not because the gifts can balance out the divine gift, but because the giving of a gift in return actually becomes a constitutive part of the reception and establishes communion. Indeed, this is why there is an intrinsically ethical dimension in the liturgy. The exercise of justice and mercy are essential dimensions of our return gift. Chauvet writes, "ethics draws its Christian aspect from its quality of a 'liturgical response'...to the initial gift of God."[26]

Attentiveness to the dynamism of gift giving and receiving in the liturgy offers yet another way to see how it is that the liturgy breaks open for us the graced character of daily living. If conventional gift exchanges belong to the world of commerce and are governed by the logic of calculation and control, the symbolic gift exchange we encounter in the liturgy disposes us to adopt a stance of radical receptivity to that which comes to us as pure gift. It demands that we abandon control so that we might truly receive. In the Eucharist, by means of sacrament, we enter into God's fundamental mode of being — gift. The celebration of the Eucharist expands our capacity to be both receptive to gift in life and also capable of *gifting* (to use Webb's neologism), in our own actions. For in the Eucharist that which we receive can be received only on the terms dictated by the Giver and not the receiver. These terms are never available to us. We cannot so construct our world as to maximize the reception of gift in predictable and reliable ways. So often, in our North American culture today, we consciously construct our world according to preconceived estimations of what is valuable and what is not. Faithful celebration of the liturgy reminds us that grace as gift can be received only as gracious and gratuitous. If I am to be open to this in-breaking of grace I must cultivate attitudes and actions that allow me to attend to the graced possibilities of daily life. These attitudes and actions will mean a repudiation of neat and arbitrary distinctions between valuable peak experiences and daily human engagements.

The Danger of Colonization

The distinctive practices of the Christian community, as we have noted, have the capacity to evangelize or reshape our world. But it would be foolish not to recognize the fact that the church has also been shaped by the values of our technological culture. In other words, to adopt the terminology of Borgmann, the liturgy too can fall prey to the influence of the device and the temptations of hyperreality.[27]

As but one example from within the Roman Catholic tradition, let us consider the confusion engendered by the present pastoral necessity of Sunday communion services in the absence of a priest. Many priests and liturgists report that significant numbers of Catholics fail to grasp the differences between a communion service and the celebration of the mass. What is of preeminent importance for many is not the actual communal performance of the eucharistic action under the presidency of a priest but rather the reception of communion. We must consider the possibility that the failure to recognize the difference reflects the colonization of liturgical sensibilities by the device paradigm. It would appear that for many Catholics, Eucharist has become a simple matter of the consumption of a sacramental "commodity" that is readily available (in the tabernacle, for example) without the "burdens" of a eucharistic action that demands the full participation (manifold engagement) of the whole people of God. Indeed one is tempted to view this attitude as simply the next step in a pattern already evident in the multiplication of the number of Sunday masses, the widespread (mis?)use of vigil masses, and the careful marketing of the liturgy to various segments of the population (for example, youth masses, children's masses, young adult masses).[28] All of these pastoral developments seek to make the grace of the sacrament ever more conveniently accessible to the believer with a minimum of disruption to the rhythms of daily life. If there is a football game on Sunday, I simply choose to attend the Saturday evening vigil mass in order to minimize the disruption of my daily life by the "burdens" of liturgical obligation.

The possible influence of the device paradigm on sacramental practice suggests a certain irony. One of the principal features of the ecclesial renewal brought about by Vatican II was the movement away from a sacramental theology shaped largely by Baroque Catholicism[29] in which theology tended to "thingify" grace and grace, in turn, was "produced" through the mechanical performance of sacramental rituals. These rituals radically separated active sacramental ministers from passive sacramental recipients. Many of the most avid proponents of the ecclesial renewal encouraged at the council are disappointed to see that this theology still remains in certain spheres of church life. Perhaps this is because they have underestimated the congeniality of this desiccated theology to modern technological society's tendency to turn human goods into commodities made ready at hand and divorced from meaningful human contexts.[30] The failure of postconciliar sacramental theology to take hold in some corners of the church may not be a mark of bad theology, tepid liturgies, or poor catechesis, but a sign of the real difficulties the church faces in evangelizing Western culture at its root, namely, the daily pattern of modern existence that is profoundly shaped by the technological paradigm.

In this chapter I have explored the fruitfulness of thinking about the liturgy as a set of "focal practices" that can help challenge the dominant ethos of North American culture, with its raging consumerism and the technological diminishment of ordinary human engagements. Karl Rahner recognized the uniquely "focal" character of the liturgy in an essay he wrote some thirty years ago. In that essay he reflected on the practice of televising masses, a practice he opposed. Certain aspects of Rahner's argument might appear quaint today, but in some respects, he anticipated our contemporary situation and offered a vision of the church as a blessed haven from the "flatness" of modern technological existence:

> Once television becomes part of the ordinary person's ordinary furniture, once he is accustomed to looking at anything and everything between heaven and earth that strikes the eye of an indiscriminately curious camera, then it is going to become an extraordinarily exciting thing, for the ordinary man [*sic*] of the twenty-first century, that there do still exist things which cannot be looked at sitting in an armchair and nibbling a sandwich. It is going to be an indescribable blessing to this man of the coming centuries, if there is still a place — the Church, in fact — where he can still retain his full natural human size; where he does not have to look at himself and his body as something archaic, a mere leftover in a world of machines with which he surrounds himself and almost tries to replace himself; where he still has a place that will continue always to heal him of his own insignificance in the midst of technology — which is indeed his task and his destiny, but can avoid being his ruin only to the degree to which he manages to retain in his life a space too, as of old, for what is merely human, what is on a small scale, what is directed bodily. There are many matters in which the Church could well be more modern than she is. But the time is beginning already in which hav-

ing the courage to be old and human is going to be the most modern thing of all.[31]

As Christians living in a technological age, we need more than ever to look to the full, conscious, and active participation in the liturgy as a means for recovering "our full natural human size." We look to the liturgy to restore for us, in short, our humanity.

Conclusion

The technological genie is out of the bottle and few are lamenting it. Indeed, the vast majority of us are far more grateful than anxious. Perhaps with some reason. After all, it is difficult not to revel in the vastly expanded freedom and range of choices that technology provides. There is no denying the intoxication that comes with new technologies or with new applications of old technologies. In countless ways modern technology has both improved the quality of and expanded the span of our lives.

Furthermore, we must resist the temptation to treat technology and Christian living as implacable foes. In profound ways the Christian religion and technology share more than we might wish to admit. Indeed a case has been made that Christianity has underwritten the Western technological impulse. Consider that, though its precise accounts vary, in one form or another the Christian economy is articulated in a basic narrative: humanity is created in the image and likeness of God and given stewardship over the created order. Humanity experiences a fall from this graced relationship with God such that the story of human history becomes now a story of both humanity estranged from itself and alienated from the created order. God's work of salvation is then conceived as the graced restoration of humanity to the divine image and likeness through the redemptive work of Christ in the power of the Spirit. From the time of the Middle Ages up to the present, the birth and development of technology (the *artes mechanicae*) were tied to this Christian economy. Technology was thought to give expression to human dominion over the created order, the restoration of the divine image in humankind, and the graced perfection of humanity.[1]

How can we not view human innovation evident in technology as an expression of imagination and intellect that are themselves marks of the divine image within us? No, our difficulty does not lie with the technological artisans. For the software designer or the electrical engineer, the invention and perfection of technological devices is doubtless itself a focal practice that expresses the ingenuity of human creativity. But the vast majority of us engage technology as consumers, not designers or inventors, and it is as consumers that we most experience technology reshaping our lives.

The best way to respond to the challenge of technology, we are tempted to believe, is with a careful assessment of the specific uses we make of technology. If the use of a home computer for on-line banking, paying bills, family budgeting, trip-planning, and pedestrian business transactions via e-mail frees me to engage in a weekend fishing trip with my children, or simply allows me more time on my front porch socializing with neighbors or passers-by (if I should be so fortunate to live in a house that still has a front porch!) the computer-as-device is being employed in service of a rich life of communion.

Just this summer, two of my children brought back from summer day camp two homing pigeons that they were to release in our neighborhood. The whole family gathered in the backyard to witness the release, and we watched with wonder as the pigeons circled above the house several times and then headed off unerringly in the direction of the camp. We decided to go on the Internet to learn more about homing pigeons and the latest theories about how they navigate. The computer and the Internet were clearly put to the service of our shared exploration.

A careful assessment of the uses of technology will help us recognize when the computer is drawing us into an endless and seductive cybernetic world of games and entertainment, untethering our relationship to the "real world" of embodied existence. When e-mail, newsgroups, chatrooms, and MUDs become the principal forum for human interaction, the device has inappropriately supplanted opportunities for authentic human engagement. When cell phones, pagers, and notebook computers are purchased in the vain hope that they can free us from the confines of the office, it is far more likely the case that they have simply *extended* office boundaries to include car and home, thereby robbing us of any remaining private space for family and recreation. This careful analysis of the particular uses of technology certainly seems reasonable. Ultimately, however, the assessment of technology must go beyond an evaluation of the uses to which devices are put.

It is a mistake to imagine that our negotiations with our technological world can take place solely on a "case-by-case" basis. Obviously, there are times when we can watch television with great benefit, make good use of computers, and have recourse to a fast food meal without any great harm. But this ignores "the pervasiveness and consistency" of the technological pattern of our lives.[2] We still need a heightened attentiveness to the overarching influence of technology and consumerism on the contours and rhythms of our daily existence. This can be accomplished only by the positive and intentional cultivation of vital focal practices that bring into relief the larger pattern of technological existence and allow us to resist its tendencies, even as we make appropriate use of technology. In other words, the discernment demanded of us is a "lifestyle" discernment, not a discernment about the goodness or badness of a particular device. It is only when I become fully aware of the technological shape of my life that I can really begin to make intentional options about how I do and do not wish to use technology. As long as the influence of technology remains invisible, there can be no meaningful lifestyle discernment.

The demanding character of this kind of lifestyle discernment has led me to a consideration of resources within the Christian tradition that may be of assistance. As Christians, our participation in the life of the church is not simply one commitment among many, and the church is not one more organization or club to which we lend our time and financial support. We believe that the Christian community offers a vital framework within which we assess all of our commitments and lifestyle choices. It is a school of discipleship, a community within which we are drawn into communion with God and communion with our neighbor. It is a community that calls us to submit ourselves to a story and a vision of human existence made concrete in the person of Jesus of Nazareth. Finally it invites us to participate in a set of ecclesial practices that engage us so fundamentally as to reorient our perspective on our daily lives.

What the church offers the world is the gospel of salvation. In Catholic teaching the church itself is the "universal sacrament of salvation."[3] By salvation we do not mean some privatized salvation of souls but an integral salvation — the salvation of humankind that embraces the personal, social, political, and economic spheres of human existence. This mission is made more difficult today, at least for the first world Christians to whom this book is primarily addressed, because one of the characteristics of modern society is the effective anesthetization of humanity to the felt need for any salvation at all. We must consider a startling paradox. By making modern daily life more "commodious" and therefore somehow "unproblematic," technology may have blinded us to the need for a careful examination of the patterns of daily life as themselves subject to conversion.[4] Consequently, the church must retrieve from its own heritage those resources best able to bring the gospel of salvation to bear on daily living. Borgmann himself noted the way in which Christ's own ministry was oriented toward the daily lives of those he encountered. Moreover, Christ's ministry "culminates in an event that engaged his followers every day, in the eucharistic meal. It is a transformed dailiness, to be sure, one that is suffused with divine love, and the focus of that transfiguration is Christ himself."[5]

As is evident by the title of this volume, I concur with Borgmann's plea for a "transformed dailiness." The Christian tradition has many names for this transformed existence: the reign of God, the life of discipleship, the state of grace, divinization, the life of communion, the imitation of Christ. At its core lies the conviction that the gospel speaks to the heart of our human existence, an existence that manifests itself more frequently in the quotidian than in the dramatic. The call to conversion is a call to a new way of life. Conversion entails, as theologian Bernard Lonergan tells us, "the transformation of horizons."[6] And this transformation begins with that most basic of horizons, daily existence.

It is this emphasis on the spiritual significance of daily existence that I believe commends the attention given to the family as a "domestic church" in Roman Catholicism over the last thirty years.[7] Unfortunately, too often discussions of "Christian families" have focused on familial structures and have tried to develop biblical or theological warrants for a divinely instituted *structure* of the family.[8] Given the wide gulf between the biblical view of the family (as an extended family with complex sociopolitical bonds that accepted polygamy and spoke little of spousal love) and the modern Western notion of the family (with its focus on the nuclear family and emphasis on spousal relationships grounded in romantic love and expressed in legal bonds) such an approach may be ill-advised. A Christian family is Christian not because it includes a father, mother, and children, but because it constitutes a shared household shaped by the values of gospel living. As Michael Lawler and Gail Risch write: "Being Christian means concretely living a Christian life. Living that life makes a family Christian, *no matter what its structure might be,* whether it be a first-century Mediterranean or twenty-first century American, whether it be nuclear or single-parent."[9]

This approach would seem to be justified by those teachings of Jesus that virtually exploded the category of the family in the ancient world. One of the most startling aspects of Jesus' teaching, and one of the things that made his teaching so distinctive, was his preaching of the coming reign of God. Jesus taught that under God's rule, kinship relations are subordinated to the spiritual bonds of discipleship. This is reflected in the important *pericope* in Mark's Gospel in which Jesus is approached by his family. When told of their arrival Jesus responds: " 'Who are my mother and my brothers and sisters?' And looking around at those seated in the circle he said, 'Here are my mother and my brothers and sisters. For whoever does the will of God is my brother and sister and mother'" (Mark 3:31–35).

The gospel of Jesus Christ stresses the creation of a new family, a new household — the household of believers. Our truest identity is discovered in the recognition that God is our Father and Mother and that we are children of God. All other relations are subordinated to this one. This teaching of Jesus need not be understood as the renunciation of the family (though Jesus apparently envisioned that some might do so "for the sake of the kingdom"). However, it does suggest that the family must now be reinterpreted in the light of the call to discipleship. If we are to remain consistent with the teaching of Jesus, our treatment of the family as domestic church must be grounded, not in blood relations that define the family but in the life of discipleship.

Consequently, when we speak of the family as domestic church I believe that our attention must be drawn not only to that constellation of relations constituted by "blood, marriage, or adoption, for the whole of life," as the American bishops recently defined the family,[10] but also to the broader notion of "household" that might include, for example, the well-known l'Arche communities founded by Jean Vanier.[11] These communities consist of large groups of the mentally handicapped who share a common household. As with the more conventional household of the nuclear family, these households center around the basic human activities of the home: sharing meals, housecleaning, bathing, getting dressed, relaxing, and conversing with others. In the context of the home we (and our children in particular) learn basic social conventions, from table manners to the demands of hospitality toward guests. In the home we learn how to be accountable for our lives; we learn when we are expected for dinner (or to prepare dinner); we learn what chores and other miscellaneous responsibilities are assigned to us and how the smooth functioning of the household depends on the fulfillment of those chores and responsibilities. More importantly, in the household we learn about the possibilities for committed intimate relationship with others and the privileges and responsibilities that those relationships bring with them.

The particular ecclesial character of the Christian household is grounded in this unique and complex set of relations realized within the home. In the complex set of relations that are realized within the household, we are engaged in the most basic of human relationships, and therefore the impact of the household on us is all the greater. This appreciation for the influence of the household in mediating values and shaping behavior coheres well with what we said earlier about the church as a school of discipleship. Indeed, Vatican II called the family or household "a school for a richer humanity" (*Gaudium et spes,* no. 52). It is in the household, where so much of daily existence transpires, that we must cultivate the "transformed dailiness" of which Borgmann speaks. For it is not by placing religious art and statuary in our homes or by saying grace at meals that the household becomes a domestic church (as valuable as those things may be). It is in the transformation of the daily patterns of the household that this community becomes itself a school of discipleship and a "domestic church."

In the Catholic Christian tradition, with its emphasis on a sacramentally constituted doctrinal teaching authority, it is not surprising that so much theological discussion is directed toward the relationship between "orthodoxy" (right belief) and "orthopraxy" (right action). Unfortunately, they are too often treated as mutually exclusive options and pitted against one another. I have written at length elsewhere about the proper relationship between the two.[12] In this volume, my concern has not been on the very real need for orthodoxy and an apostolic ministry capable of ensuring it, but rather on the dynamism of ecclesial conversion necessary if Christians are to live fruitfully or "gracefully" in the modern world. This demands a much greater concern for orthopraxis. If our technologically oriented, consumerist culture has a predilection for transforming the goods of our world into prepackaged commodities made ready-at-hand, then we Christians must look to our participation in the church (including the domestic church) and the distinctive focal practices it calls us to as a way of reorienting our lives. Consequently, I have highlighted Christian practices more than Christian doctrine. For Christian practices call us to engage our world not as consumers seeking to maximize the commodities we desire, but as children of God who seek to embrace the world as gift and strive to enter into the "gifting" dynamism of the life of grace, communion, and discipleship.

Ultimately, the call to conversion may well lead us to great decisions fraught with moral weight. It may call us to end adulterous affairs, to cease embezzling, to put aside petty hatreds. It will undoubtedly lay claim on our political commitments. It will call us to a life of compassion and justice. It will lead us to a renewed commitment to care for our planet. But these weighty decisions will be the authentic fruit and maturation of conversion only to the extent that they confirm and develop the more minute transformations realized within the interstices between these great decisions. In short, it is when "nothing is happening" that we will work out our salvation. It is only when we allow our "dailiness" to be transformed by the grace of God, that we will be able to enter into the graceful living to which people of every age have been called.

Notes

Preface

1. Albert Borgmann, *Technology and the Character of Contemporary Life* (Chicago: University of Chicago Press, 1984); *Crossing the Postmodern Divide* (Chicago: University of Chicago Press, 1992); *Holding on to Reality: The Nature of Information at the Turn of the Millennium* (Chicago: University of Chicago Press, 1999).

2. Many of the reflections offered in this book have already appeared in print in one form or another. They have all, however, been extensively reworked in this volume. I would like to acknowledge those journals that allowed me, in this volume, to draw from the following articles: "The Church as Sacrament," *The Way: Supplement,* no. 94 (1999); "Doing Liturgy in a Technological Age," *Worship* 71 (1997): 429–51; "Recovering the Sacred Mystery: How to Connect Liturgy and Life" *Modern Liturgy* 24, no. 7 (1997): 10–12 and 24, no. 8 (1997): 7–9; "The Divine in Daily Life," *America* (7 December 1996): 7–12; "North American Culture and the Liturgical Life of the Church: The Separation of the Quests for Transcendence and Community," *Worship* 68 (1994): 403–16.

1. The Technological Shape of Daily Life

1. Albert Borgmann, *Technology and the Character of Contemporary Life* (Chicago: University of Chicago Press, 1984), 40–48.

2. For beautiful meditations on feasting see both Robert Farrar Capon, *The Supper of the Lamb: A Culinary Reflec-*

tion (Garden City, N.Y.: Doubleday, 1969), and the sensual film *Babette's Feast*.

3. Borgmann, *Technology*, 196ff.

4. Ibid., 204.

5. Ibid., 42.

6. Borgmann is clearly borrowing from Alasdair Mac-Intyre's well known description of "practices": "By a 'practice' I am going to mean any coherent and complex form of socially established cooperative human activity through which the goods internal to that form of activity are realized in the course of trying to achieve those standards of excellence which are appropriate to, and partially definitive of, that form of activity, with the result that human powers to achieve excellence, and human conceptions of the ends and goods involved, are systematically extended (Alasdair MacIntyre, *After Virtue*, 2d ed. [Notre Dame: University of Notre Dame Press, 1984], 187).

7. Neil Postman, *Technopoly: The Surrender of Culture to Technology* (New York: Alfred A. Knopf, 1992), 18.

8. See Staffan Linder, *The Harried Leisure Class* (New York: Columbia University Press, 1970).

9. Umberto Eco, *Travels in Hyperreality: Essays* (San Diego: Harcourt, Brace, Jovanovich, 1986), 3–58, cited in Albert Borgmann, *Crossing the Postmodern Divide* (Chicago: University of Chicago Press, 1992), 83.

10. Ibid., 87–88.

11. Ibid., 85.

12. Ibid.

13. Hans Bernard Meyer, "Time and the Liturgy: Anthropological Notes on Liturgical Time," *Studia Liturgica* 14 (1982): 4–22.

14. See J. D. North, "Monasticism and the First Mechanical Clocks," in *The Study of Time II*, ed. J. T. Fraser and N. Lawrence (New York: Springer-Verlag, 1975), 381–98. For a perceptive treatment of the impact of the mechanical clock on modern civilization see Lewis Mumford, *Technics and Civilization* (New York: Harcourt, Brace, Jovanovich, 1963), especially chapter 2. For other helpful studies on the modern transfor-

mation of time see Stephen Jay Gould, *Time's Arrow, Time's Cycle: Myth and Metaphor in the Discovery of Geological Time* (Cambridge: Harvard University Press, 1987); S. Kern, *The Culture of Time and Space, 1880–1918* (Cambridge: Harvard University Press, 1983); Jeremy Rifkin, *Time Wars: The Primary Conflict in Human History* (New York: Henry Holt, 1987).

15. Meyer, "Time and the Liturgy," 4–7.

16. Regis Duffy, *An American Emmaus: Faith and Sacrament in the American Culture* (New York: Crossroad, 1995).

17. I am indebted to my friend Richard Nimz, computer programmer by profession, philosopher by avocation, for the significance of this distinction.

18. Borgmann, *Crossing the Postmodern Divide*, 92–93.

19. What follows draws heavily on the research of Jennifer Cypher and Eric Higgs, soon to be published in *Capitalism, Nature, Socialism,* under the title "Colonizing the Imagination: Disney's Wilderness Lodge." I am grateful to Dr. Higgs for providing me with an advance copy of their manuscript.

20. Ibid.

21. Sherry Turkle, *Life on the Screen: Identity in the Age of the Internet* (New York: Simon and Schuster, 1995), 19.

22. Ibid., 68–69.

23. Even this distinction has become blurred as computers have become for many "a second self." See Sherry Turkle, *The Second Self: Computers and the Human Spirit* (New York: Simon and Schuster, 1984).

24. Ray Oldenburg, *The Great, Good Place: Cafes, Coffee Shops, Community Centers, Beauty Parlors, General Stores, Bars, Hangouts and How They Get You through the Day* (New York: Marlowe, 1997).

25. Howard Rheingold, *Virtual Community: Homesteading on the Electronic Frontier* (New York: Addison-Wesley, 1993).

26. Ibid., italics are mine. Somewhat appropriately, this quotation is taken from the electronic version of the text, which the author has made available on the Internet.

27. This account draws from Turkle, *Life on the Screen*, 11–14. See Also Rheingold, *Virtual Community*, chapter 5.

28. Borgmann, *Crossing the Postmodern Divide*, 92.

29. Michael Heim, *The Metaphysics of Virtual Reality* (New York: Oxford University Press, 1993), 100. See also Turkle, *Life on the Screen*.

30. Ibid., 100–101.

31. Ibid., 83.

32. Michael Crichton, *Airframe* (New York: Ballantine, 1996), 422–23.

33. Borgmann, *Crossing the Postmodern Divide*, 94.

34. Ibid., 95.

35. Esther Dyson, "Put Friction Back in Cyberspace!" *Forbes ASAP* (2 December 1996): 99, 129.

36. Quoted in Neil Postman, "Science and the Story That We Need," *First Things* 69 (1997): 31.

37. Borgmann, *Technology*, 220.

38. Albert Borgmann, "Technology and the Crisis of Contemporary Culture," *American Catholic Philosophical Quarterly* 70 (1996): 41.

2. The Life of Grace

1. On the "models of God," I am indebted to Sallie McFague, *Models of God: Theology for an Ecological, Nuclear Age* (Philadelphia: Fortress, 1987).

2. Karl Rahner, "Remarks on the Dogmatic Treatise 'De Trinitate,' " in *Theological Investigations* 4 (Baltimore: Helicon Press, 1966), 79.

3. Karl Rahner, *Foundations of Christian Faith* (New York: Crossroad, 1982), 63.

4. Jim Bowman, " 'Missa Latina,' Yes, I Liked It. So Excommunicate Me," *Commonweal* 120 (8 October 1993): 6–7.

5. John D. Zizioulas, *Being as Communion* (Crestwood, N.Y.: St. Vladimir's Seminary Press, 1985).

6. For a systematic reflection on the trinitarian foundations of the life of communion see Catherine Mowry LaCugna,

God for Us: The Trinity and Christian Life (San Francisco: HarperCollins, 1991).

7. Martin Buber, *I and Thou* (New York: Charles Scribner's Sons, 1970).

8. Annie Dillard, *Pilgrim at Tinker Creek* (New York: Quality Paperbooks, 1974), 9.

9. Gerard Manley Hopkins, "God's Grandeur," *Gerard Manley Hopkins: The Major Poems,* ed. Walford Davies (London: J. M. Dent & Sons, 1979), 64.

10. Elizabeth Barrett Browning, "Aurora Leigh," in *Mrs. Browning's Complete Poetical Works,* Cambridge edition (Boston and New York: Houghton Mifflin, 1900), Book VII, lines 821–26 and 857–64.

11. Karl Rahner, "The Experience of God Today," in *Theological Investigations* 11 (London: Darton, Longman and Todd, 1974), 154.

12. Karl Rahner, "The Spirituality of the Church of the Future," in *Theological Investigations* 20 (New York: Crossroad, 1981), 149.

13. The ancient term "mystagogy" is today associated with the final stage in the Rite of Christian Initiation for Adults called *mystagogia.* It is the time between Easter and Pentecost in which the neophytes, having just celebrated the Easter sacraments, are immersed in the mysteries of the Christian faith.

14. Karl Rahner, *Belief Today* (Kansas City: Sheed & Ward, 1967), 14.

15. Kathleen Norris: *The Quotidian Mysteries: Laundry, Liturgy and "Women's Work"* (New York: Paulist, 1998), 10.

16. Ibid., 11.

17. Albert Borgmann, *Holding on to Reality: The Nature of Information at the Turn of the Millennium* (Chicago: University of Chicago Press, 1999), 177.

18. Mark Helprin, "The Acceleration of Tranquility," *Forbes ASAP* (2 December 1996): 15–22.

19. Ibid., 16.

20. Ibid.

21. Ibid.

22. Ibid., 21.

23. Dorothee Sölle, *Suffering* (Philadelphia: Fortress, 1975), 38. I hasten to add that Sölle readily admits that under certain circumstances divorce may be necessary. She is arguing against a conception of divorce that reflects our culture's unwillingness to hold to commitments when the "payoff" is not evident.

24. Ibid., 39–40.

25. Louis Bouyer, *Introduction to Spirituality* (Collegeville, Minn.: Liturgical Press, 1961), 124.

3. Toward a Communal Spirituality

1. As quoted in Louis J. Cameli, "Ecclesial Asceticism: Disciplines for the Family of Faith," *America* 175 (28 December 1996): 21.

2. Wade Clark Roof, *A Generation of Seekers: The Spiritual Journeys of the Baby Boomer Generation* (San Francisco: HarperCollins, 1993).

3. Tom Beaudoin, *Virtual Faith: The Irreverent Spiritual Quest of Generation X* (San Francisco: Jossey-Bass, 1998), 25. See also, George Barna, *Baby-Busters: The Disillusioned Generation* (Chicago: Northfield, 1994); Robert Ludwig, *Reconstructing Catholicism: For a New Generation* (New York: Crossroad, 1995).

4. For a fascinating history of the commodification of religion in America see R. Laurance Moore, *Selling God: American Religion in the Marketplace of Culture* (New York: Oxford University Press, 1994).

5. L. Gregory Jones, "A Thirst for God or Consumer Spirituality? Cultivating Disciplined Practices of Being Engaged by God," *Modern Theology* 13 (January 1997): 3–28, at 4.

6. Ibid., 6.

7. Catherine L. Albanese, "Forum," in *Religion and American Culture: A Journal of Interpretation* 1, no. 2 (1991): 138.

8. The expression "conveyor of a commodity" is taken from George Lindbeck, *The Nature of Doctrine: Religion and*

Theology in a Postliberal Age (Philadelphia: Westminster Press, 1984), 126.

9. For a penetrating analysis of the promotion of both market and nonmarket values in modern society and its impact on religion, see Alan Wolfe, *Whose Keeper? Social Science and Moral Obligation* (Berkeley: University of California Press, 1989), 27–50, and Christopher Lasch, *The True and Only Heaven: Progress and Its Critics* (New York: W. W. Norton, 1991).

10. See Moore, *Selling God*.

11. Gordon W. Lathrop, *Holy People: A Liturgical Ecclesiology* (Minneapolis: Fortress, 1999), 63.

12. See Lavinia Byrne, "An Ethic for the Internet," *The Tablet* (26 June 1999).

13. For a more sophisticated typology of the possible relationships between church and community see the 1950 classic by the Protestant theologian H. Richard Niebuhr, *Christ and Culture* (San Francisco: HarperCollins, 1986).

14. See Wayne A. Meeks, *The Origins of Christian Morality* (New Haven: Yale University Press, 1993).

15. For a beautiful theological exploration of the church as an "assembly" see Lathrop, *Holy People*.

16. Jerome Murphy-O'Connor, "Eucharist and Community in I Corinthians," in *Living Bread, Saving Cup,* ed. Kevin Seasoltz (Collegeville, Minn.: Liturgical Press, 1982), 4.

17. See Karl Rahner, "Reflections on the Unity of Love of Neighbour and the Love of God," in *Theological Investigations* 6 (New York: Crossroad, 1982), 231–52.

18. Karl Rahner, "Considerations on the Active Role of the Person in the Sacramental Event," in *Theological Investigations* 14 (New York: Seabury, 1976), 166–67.

19. Ibid., 169.

20. Michael Skelley, *The Liturgy of the World: Karl Rahner's Theology of Worship* (Collegeville, Minn.: Liturgical Press, 1991), 72.

21. Karl Rahner, "The Experience of God Today," in *Theo-*

logical Investigations 11 (London: Darton, Longman and Todd, 1974), 164–65.

22. For a very perceptive theology of preaching as the practice of "naming grace" in the lives of believers see Mary Catherine Hilkert, *Naming Grace: Preaching and the Sacramental Imagination* (New York: Continuum, 1997).

23. Hilkert, *Naming Grace,* 81ff. See also Richard R. Gaillardetz, "In Service of Communion: A Trinitarian Foundation for Christian Ministry," *Worship* 67 (September 1993): 418–33.

24. Albert Borgmann, "Technology and the Crisis of Contemporary Culture," *American Catholic Philosophical Quarterly* 70 (1996): 42.

25. Norman Maclean, *A River Runs through It* (Chicago: University of Chicago Press, 1976), 1–4.

26. Borgmann, looking to premodern religion, defined "sacred practices" in this way: "A sacred practice...consisted in the regular reenactment of the founding act, and so it renewed and sustained the order of the world. Christianity came into being this way; the eucharistic meal, the Supper of the Lamb, is its central event, established with the instruction that it be reenacted" (Borgmann, *Technology,* 207).

27. Stephen H. Webb, *The Gifting God: A Trinitarian Ethics of Excess* (New York and Oxford: Oxford University Press, 1996), 93.

28. Ibid., 93–94.

4. Liturgy of the Church, Liturgy of the World

1. See Alexander Schmemann, *For the Life of the World,* rev. ed. (Crestwood, N.Y.: St. Vladimir's Press, 1973), 24–26.

2. Ibid., 27.

3. See Ion Bria, *The Liturgy after the Liturgy* (Geneva: World Council of Churches, 1996).

4. See Karl Rahner, "On the Theology of Worship," in *Theological Investigations* 19 (New York: Crossroad, 1983), 141–49; idem, "Considerations on the Active Role of the Per-

son in the Sacramental Event," in *Theological Investigations* 14 (New York: Seabury, 1976), 161–84. See also Michael Skelley, *The Liturgy of the World: Karl Rahner's Theology of Worship* (Collegeville, Minn.: Liturgical Press, 1991).

5. Gordon Lathrop, *Holy Things: A Liturgical Theology* (Minneapolis: Fortress, 1993), 90.

6. "Bread and wine are already sacred things before their use by Christians" (ibid., 93).

7. Louis-Marie Chauvet refers to this as a "symbolic rupture" in *Symbol and Sacrament: A Sacramental Reinterpretation of Christian Existence* (Collegeville, Minn.: Liturgical Press, 1995), 330–39.

8. Victor Turner refers to this state of disorientation as "liminality." See "Passages, Margins and Poverty: Religious Symbols of Communitas," *Worship* 46 (1972): 399.

9. Nathan Mitchell, "The Sense of the Sacred," in *Parish: A Place for Worship,* ed. Mark Searle (Collegeville, Minn.: Liturgical Press, 1981), 80.

10. Theodore Jennings, "On Ritual Knowledge," *Journal of Religion* 62 (1982): 115.

11. Ibid., 116, 118.

12. Susan J. White perceptively considers the implications of changing technologies of time-keeping for the liturgy in *Christian Worship and Technological Change* (Nashville: Abingdon Press, 1994), 64–70.

13. For a wonderful reflection on the liturgical transformation of time see Alexander Schmemann, *For the Life of the World,* rev. ed. (Crestwood, N.Y.: St. Vladimir's Seminary Press, 1973), 48ff.

14. Regis Duffy, *An American Emmaus: Faith and Sacrament in the American Culture* (New York: Crossroad, 1995), 96.

15. Stanislaus Campbell, "Hours, Liturgy of the Day," in *The New Dictionary of Sacramental Worship,* ed. Peter E. Fink (Collegeville, Minn.: Liturgical Press, 1990), 575.

16. Irmgard Pahl, "The Paschal Mystery in its Central Mean-

ing for the Shape of Christian Liturgy," *Studia Liturgica* 26 (1996): 16–38.

17. Nathan Mitchell, "Liturgical Correctness," *Worship* 71 (1977): 62–71, at 71.

18. Patrick T. McCormick, "How Could We Break the Lord's Bread in a Foreign Land? The Eucharist in 'Diet America,' " *Horizons* 25 (1998): 43–57, at 44–45. This section draws heavily on McCormick's article.

19. Ibid., 50–53. See also Michelle Stacey, *Why Americans Love, Hate and Fear Food* (New York: Simon and Schuster, 1994).

20. McCormick, "How Could We Break the Lord's Bread in a Foreign Land?" 52.

21. From an address by Fr. Robert Hovda given at a Catholic Worker house in May 1983.

22. McCormick, "How Could We Break the Lord's Bread in a Foreign Land?" 50.

23. What follows draws on the dense but rewarding reflection on the dynamisms of symbolic exchange, graciousness, and gratuity in Chauvet, *Symbol and Sacrament*, 99–109. I am grateful to Richard Fragomeni for suggesting the helpfulness of Chauvet's work for my own project.

24. Ibid., 108.

25. For this phrase and the meditation that follows, see Daniel W. Hardy and David F. Ford, *Praising and Knowing God* (Philadelphia: Westminster, 1985), 6.

26. Chauvet, *Symbol and Sacrament*, 281. For a helpful reflection on the ethical dimensions of the sacraments, see Timothy F. Sedgwick, *Sacramental Ethics: Paschal Mystery and the Christian Life* (Philadelphia: Fortress, 1987).

27. Moving along a parallel track, Susan White reflects on the influence of "mechanistic thinking" on the experience of worship. See White, *Christian Worship and Technological Change*, 101–3.

28. The salient characteristics of this liturgical tendency are disclosed in a more dramatic form in the rise in some Protestant churches of "seeker services" in which liturgical wor-

ship, the "summit and font" of Christian life, is transformed into a quasi-marketing tool for evangelical outreach to the newest generation of spiritual "seekers." For an analysis of the "seeker service" phenomenon and the related "church growth" movement, see Frank C. Senn, " 'Worship Alive': An Analysis and Critique of 'Alternative Worship Services,' " *Worship* 69 (1995): 194–224; Lester Ruth, *"Lex Agendi, Lex Orandi:* Toward an Understanding of Seeker Services as a New Kind of Liturgy," *Worship* 71 (1996): 386–405.

29. See Thomas F. O'Meara, "Leaving the Baroque: The Fallacy of Restoration in the Postconciliar Era," *America* 174 (3 February 1996): 10–14, 25–28.

30. Borgmann makes a similar observation in "Technology and the Crisis of Contemporary Culture," *American Catholic Philosophical Quarterly* 70 (1996): 41–42.

31. Karl Rahner, "The Mass and Television," in *The Christian Commitment: Essays in Pastoral Theology* (New York: Sheed & Ward, 1963), 217.

Conclusion

1. See David F. Noble, *The Religion of Technology: The Divinity of Man and the Spirit of Invention* (New York: Penguin Books, 1999).

2. Albert Borgmann, *Technology and the Character of Contemporary Life* (Chicago: University of Chicago Press, 1984), 208.

3. See *Lumen gentium,* no. 15; *Gaudium et spes,* no. 45.

4. Albert Borgmann, "Prospects for the Theology of Technology," in *Theology and Technology: Essay in Christian Analysis and Exegesis,* ed. Carl Mitcham and Jim Grote (Lanham, Md.: University Press of America, 1984), 307.

5. Albert Borgmann, "Christianity and the Cultural Center of Gravity," *Listening* 18 (1983): 93–102, at 99–100.

6. See Bernard Lonergan, *Method in Theology,* reprint ed. (Toronto: University of Toronto Press, 1990).

7. Among the documents of Vatican II, see *Lumen gen-*

tium, no. 11; *Apostolicam actuositatem,* no. 11. Among post-conciliar magisterial documents of the Catholic Church see Pope Paul VI, "Apostolic Exhortation on Evangelization in the Modern World" (*Evangelii nuntiandi*), (Washington, D.C.: USCC, 1976), no. 71; Pope John Paul II, "Apostolic Exhortation on the Family" (*Familiaris consortio*) *Origins* 11 (24 December 1981): no. 39.

8. See Michael G. Lawler and Gail S. Risch, "Covenant Generativity: Toward a Theology of Christian Family," *Horizons* 26 (1999): 7–30.

9. Ibid., 17, italics in the original.

10. NCCB Ad Hoc Committee on Marriage and Family Life, *A Family Perspective in Church and Society* (Washington, D.C.: U.S. Catholic Conference, 1998), 19.

11. See Jean Vanier, *Community and Growth* (New York: Paulist Press, 1989); Michael Downey, *A Blessed Weakness: The Spirit of Jean Vanier and l'Arche* (San Francisco: Harper and Row, 1986).

12. See Richard R. Gaillardetz, *Teaching with Authority: A Theology of the Magisterium in the Church* (Collegeville, Minn.: Liturgical Press, 1997).